Dynamic Dialogues

Dynamic Dialogues

A Human-Centered Approach to Navigate the Flaws of Feedback

Melissa Versino

Tampa, Florida

The views and opinions expressed in this book are solely those of the author and do not reflect the views or opinions of Gatekeeper Press. Gatekeeper Press is not to be held responsible for and expressly disclaims responsibility for the content herein.

Dynamic Dialogues: A Human-Centered Approach to Navigate the Flaws of Feedback

Published by Gatekeeper Press
7853 Gunn Hwy, Suite 209
Tampa, FL 33626
www.GatekeeperPress.com

Copyright © 2023 by Melissa Versino
All rights reserved. Neither this book, nor any parts within it may be sold or reproduced in any form or by any electronic or mechanical means, including information storage and retrieval systems, without permission in writing from the author. The only exception is by a reviewer, who may quote short excerpts in a review.

Library of Congress Control Number: 2023938067

ISBN (paperback): 9781662937804
eISBN: 9781662937811

Contents

Introduction vii

Chapter One: Feedback Defined 1
- What Is Feedback?   1
- Biological Need for Feedback   2
- An Unavoidable Obstacle?   5

Chapter Two: Why We Give Feedback 6
- Who Does the Feedback Benefit?   7
- Feedback in Principle   9

Chapter Three: How We Deliver Feedback 18
- Feedback Models   18
- Where the Models are Lacking   22

Chapter Four: Feedback Initiatives Within
Organizations 25
- Organizational Feedback Efforts   25
- Feedback Loops   27

Chapter Five: Fundamental Feedback Flaws 31
- The Six Flaws of Feedback   31
- Fundamentally Flawed… A Summary   47

Chapter Six: The Lasting Impact Feedback Can Have ... 48
- A Gift 48
- Feedback Fallout 49
- Disproportionate Impact on Women 64
- Diversity Lost? 67
- Conditioning our Feedback Response 68

Chapter Seven: Expert Advice on How to Improve Feedback Experience 70
- The Secret Sauce? 70
- Building on Expert Advice 79

Chapter Eight: How a Coaching Approach is a Step in the Right Direction 80
- What Is Coaching? 80
- Why Coaching? 83
- Coaching in Principle 86
- Coaching Models 90
- Coaching and Feedback 92

Chapter Nine: Creating Dynamic Dialogues 95
- Flip the Focus 95
- Empathetic Inquiry 97
- Let's Talk! 99
- Why Give Feedback When You Can Just Talk? 111
- Now What? 114

Conclusion 117

References 121

Introduction

Feedback is a powerful tool intended to spark improvement in behavior or performance. Unfortunately, there are many flaws inherent to feedback that impede our desired outcomes and limit the potential of others. Rather than inspire self-reflection and confidence, the result of feedback is often reliance on more feedback and triggering of our innate threat response systems. By taking a more human-centered approach to cultivate **dynamic dialogues** with people, we can reduce the amount of stress and negative consequences of feedback in both our personal and professional lives.

In this book we'll ...

... explore the theory and modalities of feedback while exposing the reality of feedback in practice. This **reality gap** will be discussed in detail, allowing a deeper understanding where feedback is lacking.

... highlight the **fundamental feedback flaws** and look at expert advice on how to address those flaws to create a better feedback experience.

... uncover the **lasting impact** that just one negative experience can have on us.

... discuss how ***coaching*** can begin to address some of the flaws of feedback and think about how to expand the ability to mitigate those challenges even further.

... talk about the fascinating ***brain science*** supporting how to engage in positive discussions.

... find a way to talk to each other and share perspectives to move forward and ***inspire deeper self-reflection and awareness.***

With over thirty years of experience in corporate America, I have seen the good, bad, and ugly sides of leadership and envision a world where leaders lead through inspiration and not intimidation. My commitment to unlocking the boundless potential of others led me to become a coach. As a result of my experience coaching others as well as through the process of earning several formal coaching certifications, I have become attuned to the power of coaching.

My personal experience with feedback, as well as years of hearing feedback horror stories unfold and providing support to recovering feedback receivers, made me question feedback overall. I questioned why we give feedback, what the purpose is, and why it's so hard to do it well. This compelled me to conceive a better way of exchanging perspectives to achieve better self-improvement outcomes.

This book is for you if you have ever received feedback that made you angry or frustrated. I'm willing to bet that just like many other people I've talked to, you've had a negative experience with feedback. Whether you disagreed with it, didn't like how the message was delivered, or didn't trust or

Introduction

respect the person providing you with the feedback, likely it stuck with you, and if asked you could recall exactly how you felt in that moment. Perhaps it stayed with you for years, and you altered your behavior in a way that doesn't feel true to you.

Whether you are a professional, parent, or anyone else, you are probably in situations where you need to share your thoughts with someone to encourage a different behavior from them.

If you cringe at the thought of "feedback," this book is for you. We'll explore what feedback is, why and how we do it, and more. You'll learn new techniques to reevaluate how to share your perspective and create a more compelling conversation with others rather than a discouraging confrontation.

CHAPTER ONE

Feedback Defined

"I have some feedback for you." What does it feel like to hear those words? What response does it elicit from you? We've all been in situations where someone provided feedback to us and we likely can recall that memory and how we felt in that moment. And often that memory probably includes feelings such as stress, anxiety, frustration, anger, and even denial. Even in the best of situations, feedback is hard to receive and to give.

What Is Feedback?

Let's start by defining what feedback is. Feedback is the act of providing information to someone to evaluate and correct performance, behavior, processes, or events. Seems innocent enough, right? Ironically, another way we think of feedback is when we hear that screech or hum from a device, such as a microphone or amplifier, when it feeds back into itself. I've been in some situations where feedback felt much more like the second definition than the first. You may have seen a cartoon, meme, GIF, or other graphic that represents a teacher speaking to a classroom where everyone is tuned out and their actual words can't be processed by the students other than as "blah, blah, blah," or something of the like. Or you likely have experienced this yourself as what someone is saying to you becomes just a wordless hum you are not able to decipher. Or even worse, when feedback feels like a painful screeching noise.

Feedback is a tool used within professional organizations, educational institutions, and personal relationships to provide information about another's behavior or actions with the intent of changing, stopping, or improving that behavior or action. Feedback is valuable and helps to provide external perspectives to help limit blind spots and better understand the impact we're having on others. Feedback is a necessary input into personal and professional development.

Biological Need for Feedback

Feedback also is a biological imperative for our species to survive and evolve. "Feedback isn't just a ritual of the modern workplace. It is a means by which organisms, across a variety of life-forms and time periods, have adapted to survive. To University scientist Tom Stafford, feedback is the essence of intelligence."[1]

Our bodies require feedback to inform our internal systems and processes to preserve homeostasis, which is the process of maintaining a steady state. Our systems attempt to regulate biological and chemical processes within our body to achieve homeostasis and keep everything operating effectively and in balance. Just like an instrument panel on a car or airplane, our bodies are tracking and measuring information that is valuable for us to understand whether we're maintaining that steady state or adjustments are needed.

Feedback Defined

To enable homeostasis, there are several components necessary to receive, process, and react to internal and external feedback. The stimulus is the information, or feedback, component which signals that something is moving away from the expected range. The sensor acts as a monitor to evaluate the stimulus and send data to the control center, which then compares how the stimulus is performing to normal, expected values of performance. If the control center identifies that there is performance outside of the normal range, it will signal the effector which responds to the signal to return to the expected range. Within our bodies the effectors are muscles, glands, organs, or other similar structures.[2]

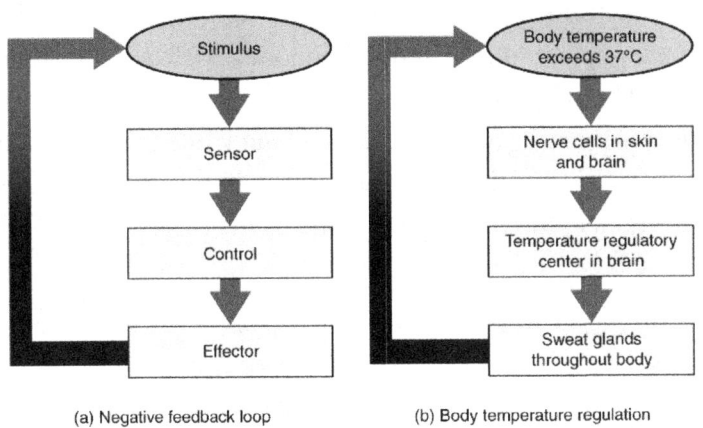

(a) Negative feedback loop   (b) Body temperature regulation

Homeostasis & Feedback: *how external stimulus initiates our negative feedback loop*[3]

Consider you've just placed your hand on a hot stove burner. You will almost immediately remove your hand to avoid a painful burn. In this example, the hot stove is the stimuli. The nerves within the body that sense the heat transmit a signal to your brain with information. Your brain then processes that information and relays a message back to the muscles in your hand to move so that you do not experience further damage. Just like we are thirsty when we need water and tired when we need sleep, this type of feedback is critical, and our bodies and brains need to be able to respond in a way that keeps us safe and maintains homeostasis.

Feedback also plays a role in Darwin's theory of evolution in the mechanism of natural selection, which describes how species adapt over time to be better suited to their environments, or as their environments change. All species rely on receiving information about their environment and from within their bodies. You may be familiar with the image below, of giraffes with shorter and longer necks. Depending on the food available in its environment, a giraffe with a longer neck would be better equipped to find and obtain food. So, from a biological perspective, we need information for our continued survival. This is happening at a genetic level, and while this is not quite the same as receiving feedback from another person on our performance, the underlying theme is the same.

Representation of Natural Selection: *gradual change in traits in the giraffe population (long-necked giraffes survive and reproduce) as a result of being able to reach food that is unreachable otherwise*[4]

An Unavoidable Obstacle?

So, if feedback is necessary and valuable personally, professionally, and biologically, what's the problem? Consider feedback as information or input from our environment. Whether it's to help us survive as a species or thrive in our relationships and careers, it's something that is needed for us to learn, grow, and evolve. As vital as getting input is for our survival, this is at odds with how our bodies perceive and respond to feedback we receive in social and professional situations. While we need this external, and internal, information to keep ourselves in balance and make necessary adjustments for sustained performance, we also perceive the information itself as a threat. We'll explore that a bit further later, for now let's look at some ways we deliver feedback.

CHAPTER TWO

Why We Give Feedback

Feedback is meant to be positive and given with the purpose of improving something or someone. We offer feedback to others with the intent of helping them. Feedback is offered to move someone from an undesirable behavior to a more acceptable alternative action. The question is, who decides what's undesirable and what's acceptable? In the case of feedback, it's usually the feedback giver. What makes them particularly qualified to make that determination, you might ask. It could be that they have more experience or knowledge. Or it could be just a matter of opinion or perspective, yet feedback tends to be viewed as fact while it is a perception. We then say "perception is reality," which is true for each person but may not be the same across many people.

When we have a certain level of knowledge or expertise, of course we should use that to teach and help others. This is particularly meaningful and necessary in the case of technical skill development. In some things there is a clear right and wrong way to do something, but also as technology and our skills evolve, the right way may not be the only way, or even the right way forever. In part, this is what makes feedback not necessarily always a fact that can be used to determine the "right" way.

Who Does the Feedback Benefit?

While feedback is intended to help someone, I would ask who is the someone it's intended to help. Is it the person whose behavior is undesirable, or is it the people who are on the receiving end of that behavior? Could it be both? The reality is that via sharing our perspective we are seeking to help that person minimize the negative impact they are having on others, which in turn could improve their relationships and performance. But the focus can be more on the how do you make this better for *me*, rather than how can you make this better for *you*. Which flips the intention from being altruistic to being more self-serving.

The next time you have feedback to share with someone, stop to think about it a moment. What purpose do you have for providing your thoughts to the person? There can be many, such as you want to increase their awareness, they are doing something that doesn't benefit you, others, or themselves, you are frustrated by their behavior, or they made a mistake and need to resolve it. So, in the end, who is the feedback serving the most?

In this way, feedback tends to be very much about the receiver and what they need to do to make it better for others. Our intentions are good, we do want to help them, but we are also seeking to help eliminate something that we don't like or doesn't help us. The irony is that often we discover through feedback that a person's actions didn't match their intentions; the same can be true of giving feedback. The intention to help someone may not always be best served by offering feedback, even if following a model and operating at least to some extent within the principles we'll explore below.

Understanding the purpose of feedback and finding a model to help structure the feedback is a good start. Where it falls short is that each of the models only consider certain principles that make feedback effective but do not seem to incorporate them all. And just like in building a house, you need to know what you're trying to accomplish and understand which tools to use (models), but without understanding the principles of building a house you're missing a piece of the puzzle. Think of it like understanding the architecture and where load-bearing support structures are needed, the flow of the plumbing and electric, and the best material to use given the climate. Without this knowledge, without a clear blueprint, the right tools and material can only get you so far.

Understanding the principles of feedback can help provide clarity to guide us. However, some principles can also create confusion if not applied as intended or fit for purpose. A principle is a fundamental truth that acts as a foundation of a system of belief or behavior. In most cases the feedback principles are sound in theory but in practice something gets lost in translation. This is where it could be better to focus on the intent of each principle and follow the spirit of the law rather than the letter of the law. Let's get into the key principles around giving feedback and explore the intent and how these can lead toward ineffective feedback if applied too strictly.

Feedback in Principle

Principle #1: Feedback should be balanced. Feedback should include elements of positive input that recognize and praise, as well as constructive input that identifies opportunities for improvement. According to research, the ideal positive to constructive feedback ratio is 5:1. Meaning for every constructive comment you make, you need to share five positive comments. This stems from research in the 1970s and '80s, into the magic ratio of good relationships, by psychologists John Gottman, PhD, and Robert Levenson, PhD. Their studies suggested there is a ratio of five positive interactions for every one negative interaction in successful, long-lasting relationships. Couples with lower than the 5:1 ratio were more likely to be divorced in the future.[5] Further work into this ratio by Marcial Losada and Emily Heaphy was done in a business setting. Their observations also highlighted better performance in teams that had a higher ratio of positive to negative comments.[6]

In theory, this makes sense. Constant criticism wears away at our confidence and diminishes us while praise can lift us and increase our confidence. However, in practice, a few things tend to happen when applying this principle. This can turn into a feedback "sandwich," where the constructive criticism is sandwiched between two praises. This was taught in many feedback training sessions, and I've had the opportunity to see how this approach plays out and generally see two things. One, the feedback around what needs to be changed gets buried and lost, and two, the message is unclear, often leading the feedback receiver to focus only on the message they most likely want to hear, which are the positive comments. While this principle is valuable, it is just an overarching way to think about how you provide your perspective and insights to others, which should generally not be balanced but actually disproportionately skewed toward positive reinforcement and feedback at a 5:1 ratio. The concept here is to that provide positive reinforcement more often than constructive criticism, and as we explore how to have more dynamic dialogues, we can apply this concept in the form of acknowledging both the strengths and challenges of others in a way that validates them.

Principle #2: **Ask permission before giving feedback.** This is another principle that seems sound and logical. Before you offer your perspective (generally criticism) of someone to them, make sure they want to hear it. But what does this mean in practice? At times it's extremely helpful to ask whether someone is interested in hearing your perspective and feedback. But what if you are managing a team and need to provide performance feedback to ensure goals are met and the team member is meeting expectations, do you ask the team member if they want your feedback? What if they say no? Do you offer it anyway because they need to hear it? In my experience, I see this fundamentally making sense to ask something like, "May I offer my perspective?" or "Can I share my thinking with you?" when appropriate. Or even ask, "When would be a good time to discuss how that meeting went?" In this way you are giving some control to the feedback receiver, but be clear on how much say they really have in whether they want to hear the feedback or not. There are certainly times when this would be more appropriate. But it's all about understanding the intent of this principle, which is to make sure the person is in the best state of mind possible to receive the feedback and may decline feedback that is not essential for them. The other concept that goes along with this is that as a giver of feedback, it's up to you to determine whether the feedback is really needed, and ask yourself how this information or perspective will help the other person. If there's not a valid reason to provide that feedback, then don't share it and you won't need to ask for permission.

Principle #3: A feedback conversation should be exactly that, a conversation. This requires dialogue between two (or more) people to move the discussion forward. This is a principle that I agree with in theory and practice, yet application of this principle tends to fall short. Some of this ties to the feedback models we will review in a bit, but you'll see that not all models incorporate a two-way discussion, and because generally giving and receiving feedback is uncomfortable at best, the feedback giver tends to want to just get it out and follow the model structure to deliver the message as quickly as possible. The dialogue part is crucial to an effective feedback discussion and yet often overlooked or insubstantial. And not only that, but often we teach people that they need to receive feedback in an open way, and they should take it and process it without explaining why they behaved a certain way, or they will come off as defensive. Where does that leave them? They must learn to tactfully listen, absorb, ask questions, understand, and explain themselves in a way that doesn't get perceived as self-justifying or close-minded. Not easy, right?

Principle #4: Feedback should be specific. Another great principle intended to ensure that there is as much clarity in the feedback as possible to provide context. Often, feedback is very general and non-specific; for example, "Really great job today." While that may feel good to be praised, it's not clear exactly what went well today, or what specific behaviors or accomplishments should be repeated or built upon. That is where this principle really helps drive more details around what specifically went well, or didn't, as compared to those general statements lacking clarity. Where I've seen this go wrong runs along the spectrum of omitting specific details entirely on one end to providing so much detail that the actual feedback gets lost in the minutiae at the other end. It's important to consider how much detail and specifics are needed to provide an understanding of the situation, event, and behavior while not overwhelming someone.

Principle #5: When possible, the person giving the feedback should directly observe the behavior or situation. It is key to not provide feedback based purely on hearsay. This principle is intended to ensure that people aren't simply passing along rumors or things that have been overheard as feedback. Just like the other principles, there should be some flexibility in how this is applied. There may be times when the person giving the feedback did not directly observe a situation but is in the best position to provide feedback to someone. This happens often with parents, who have a direct responsibility for their child, or managers, who have a direct responsibility for their team members. In other situations, there may not be trust or a relationship between the person who observed the situation and the person who is receiving the feedback, and it may be better delivered by someone else. It's good to challenge that, however, and if someone comes to me to talk about one of my team members, I ask what they have shared with the team member directly and encourage them to do so. I can follow up and provide additional perspective and chat about how to move forward and where I can support them. Overall, the goal is to consider who is the best person to deliver this feedback and how to encourage the person who observed the situation to provide the feedback directly. This also is intended to help the feedback be as accurate as possible, which is more likely when observed by the giver and not shared through others (think of the game of "telephone" where messages get mixed up as it goes from person to person to person).

Principle #6: Feedback should incorporate alternative actions. This provides alternative options to replace the undesired behavior by providing an idea of more acceptable behaviors. This is another principle that is very beneficial and should be part of any feedback discussion. However, where this falls flat is that these alternatives tend to be offered by the feedback giver rather than generated by the feedback receiver. This is usually done with good intention and offered in the way that the feedback giver would have done it. What this doesn't take into consideration is that each of us is a unique person and what works for you may not work for me. It also usually puts the feedback receiver as the owner of an action or solution that they didn't have a part in coming up with, which leads to lower self-accountability for that action. When asked as a question rather than immediately offered as an idea, this works rather well. Instead of offering a specific solution, ask something like, "What could you have done differently?" or "What are some other ways you could approach that situation?" This allows the person receiving the feedback to be a part of the discussion and find a solution that works best for themselves, and as the feedback giver you can provide insights on whether that could work or ask what other ideas they have. Many times, this is not the approach taken and leaves the feedback receiver feeling like they were reprimanded and must do what they are told rather than absorbing and personalizing the feedback and choosing the resulting actions for themselves.

Principle #7: *Be objective in the feedback, refrain from making assumptions or judgments.* This links well with the prior principle requiring feedback to be given as a result of directly observing a behavior. Although it's safe to say just because it was directly observed, doesn't mean that it is objective and free from biases, assumptions, or judgments. This is a sound principle but tends to be difficult to execute, as I mentioned earlier. Our nature as humans is to make assumptions and fill in the gaps in our understanding. It's really challenging to be objective and rather, we tend to assume we know why the person did what they did and that we know the best way to approach something. This may be the case, but it also may not be, and without challenging our objectivity and asking ourselves how much we know as fact and what assumptions we are making, this principle is unmet.

We also make value judgments suggesting to us that the behavior we observed was either "right" or "wrong." We tend to put our assumptions into these "good" and "bad" buckets to allow us to categorize and process them. In my experience, this is the most difficult feedback flaw to overcome due to our human nature. It requires us to both acknowledge and push past our initial assumptions and judgments to approach with curiosity instead. And to recognize we don't have to agree or even understand a person's motivation or rationale to validate them. It's helpful here to acknowledge that while someone else's behaviors, thoughts, and emotions may not be aligned with ours, that doesn't make them wrong or bad necessarily.

Principle #8: Provide timely feedback. This is a principle that should be straightforward but can be challenging to apply. Ideally the timing of when feedback is delivered should be reasonably close to the event or behavior that was observed. The first question would be, how would you define within a "reasonable" period? There's no magic right answer to this, and I've found that some people want this as soon as you can possibly deliver the feedback, and others may prefer sometime within the next week or so, connected to a regular discussion or one-on-one meeting that is already scheduled. There is a bit of vagueness in how soon is within a timely manner. While there isn't a magic right answer, there is a wrong one, and that is waiting "too long" after the event to deliver the feedback. Again, the challenge is determining how long is "too long." A classic example that I've seen too many times to count is waiting to deliver feedback related to behaviors impacting performance until a formal performance review, which traditionally happens only once or twice a year. The gap between the observation and feedback could be months in this case. When not shared sooner, two outcomes are likely: The ability to recall the specific event or behavior with clarity may be diminished for both parties, and the feedback receiver isn't able to absorb the feedback and adjust behavior before there are performance implications. This creates frustration or surprise often paired with a protest of "if you only told me sooner, I could have done something differently."

Principle #9: Approach feedback with kindness. This is connected to an important component of feedback from my perspective, which is empathy. You may be familiar with the quote, "THINK before you speak. Is it True, Helpful, Inspiring, Necessary, Kind?"[7] by Alan Redpath, a British evangelist, pastor, and author. This is a great way to formulate feedback as well. The questions this leaves me with are what is kind and what if the feedback you want to share may be hurtful to someone, do you refrain from sharing that? The desire to be kind often results in avoiding the discussion, tiptoeing around the concern or issue, or clouding the message. Kindness is characterized by being friendly, generous, and considerate. It's a key quality to have in giving feedback, and I would push even further to think about empathy, really seeking to understand and even share the feelings of another person.

Are you familiar with the saying, "if you don't have anything nice to say, don't say anything at all"? This is something many of us were taught early on and treat as a golden rule even into our adulthood. This was particularly helpful as children learning how to keep our opinions to ourselves. This adage may be responsible for people shying away from providing negative or constructive feedback to others. They think, well, I don't have anything nice to say, so I might as well not say it. While this can be somewhat of a litmus test in terms of how you should consider providing the feedback, it isn't a very effective indicator on its own of whether to provide feedback to someone or not. Without the other elements that THINK provides, such as could what you share be helpful to the person in exposing a blind spot or helping to broaden their understanding, it would be easy to put all constructive feedback in the "nothing nice to say" bucket and call it a day.

CHAPTER THREE

How We Deliver Feedback

There are many models that can be used to structure and deliver feedback. Each model can be beneficial and it's really a matter of preference. Some of these models are outlined below, but there are many others. For each model, let's take a simple example scenario and play out the feedback. Let's say you are in a team meeting and John, one of your team members, is checking his cell phone throughout the meeting and isn't participating in the discussion.

Feedback Models

The first model we'll look at is **SBIA**, which stands for Situation, Behavior, Impact, and Action/Alternative. I've had a lot of experience using this model both personally to deliver feedback and as part of our leadership development programs and have seen it as SBI as well. I prefer the addition of the A for action or alternative because the desired output of feedback is to understand what to do differently, and without that component it's lacking. In this model, the feedback provider shares the specific situation, highlights the behavior that is unwanted, describes the impact the behavior had on themselves and/or others, and the alternative or action to be taken, if incorporated. Using the example scenario, it would sound something like this:

"John, I have some feedback for you. In yesterday's team meeting (situation), you were checking your phone several times and didn't engage in the discussion (behavior). You seemed really distracted and you didn't pay attention to the rest of the team or contribute your own ideas. This felt disrespectful to your team members (impact). Please keep your phone from distracting you during team meetings and disrupting your team members (alterative action)."

Overall, the message was straightforward, and John would know what was expected of him in team meetings. However, John didn't necessarily share his own perspectives and could be left feeling scolded.

Next, we'll explore **STAR/AR**, which represents Situation, Task, Action, Result, Alternative, Result. Here we begin with describing the situation, the specific task the person did, the action they chose, and the result of that action. If desired, an alternative action and alternative result of that action can also be incorporated. This is another simple model to utilize, though it can be a bit unclear or duplicative between the situation, task, and action elements. This model may be better served in a highly transactional setting given the focus on task completion. Applying this model to the above scenario would sound like this:

"John, I have some feedback for you. During the team meeting yesterday (situation), you were not able to focus or participate (task) because you were on your phone several times during the meeting (action). The result is that you didn't contribute anything, didn't hear what we were discussing, and didn't show respect for your team members' time and thoughts (result). In the future during team meetings, I would like you to put your phone away and be fully present during team meetings (alternative action) so that you can effectively listen and contribute to the discussion (alternative result)."

Again, this model is straightforward and simple enough that John would know not to bring his phone into meetings so that he can participate.

Let's look at the **BEST** feedback model, representing Behavior, Effects, Stop, and Take next steps. In this model the feedback giver should focus on the specific behavior that occurred, how that behavior impacted others, stop to allow for a dialogue, and then discuss what should happen next as a result of the feedback given.

For example, "John, I'd like to give you some feedback. You were on your phone several times during the team meeting and as a result didn't participate or listen to your team members. What do you think about that?" This could open for some dialogue to hear John's reaction or thoughts. "Ok, let's discuss what should happen next. In the future, I need you to actively participate in team meetings and not be distracted by your phone, can you commit to that?" Again, allowing for some dialogue. This approach allows for the interaction between feedback giver and receiver, which is great, but depending on how the discussion goes that interaction may not be productive or feel like a true dialogue.

Another model that incorporates an opportunity for integrating a dialogue is the **OEPS** model, which stands for Observation, Effect, Pause, and Suggest. Using this approach, the feedback giver shares one observed behavior, explains the outcome of that behavior, pauses to prompt a dialogue by staying silent, and finally prompts the receiver to discuss alternative behaviors if they don't get to this on their own.

Putting this to action, here's our example scenario: "Hi John, I have some feedback I'd like to discuss with you. I observed you looking at your phone several times during our team meeting yesterday (observation). Because you were focused on your phone you missed a good part of the discussion and didn't participate actively (effect)." Here we'd pause and wait for John to share his thoughts, and if he doesn't, prompt him with a question like, "What do you think?" At this point John would share his thoughts, and perhaps we'd get into a bit more about what caused him to be on his phone, but that would depend on how we direct the dialogue. Lastly, if John doesn't share his thoughts on what to do instead, we'd ask, "What could you do differently next time?" The benefit to this model is it allows for dialogue and for the feedback receiver to be the one who suggests the alternative action rather than the feedback giver, which creates personal accountability to the solution.

The last model to explore is **BOOST**, which stands for Balanced, Observed, Objective, Specific, and Timely. The purpose of this model is to ensure that the feedback is balanced, with a mix of both constructive and positive feedback. The feedback given should be something directly observed, not hearsay, and should be based on what happened, not your interpretation of it. Feedback should also be specific and as accurate as possible and given timely, as close to the observed behavior as possible to make it relevant and more likely the feedback receiver will recall the situation clearly. For me these are more like the underlying principles for feedback rather than a model or framework to structure a specific piece of feedback, although I would include a few other principles.

Let's try it anyway, it would go something like this: "John, let's talk about some feedback I have for you. Thank you for being on time for the team meeting earlier today. I noticed that you were checking your phone throughout the meeting. I specifically saw at least three instances where I looked over at you and you were focused on your phone. You usually contribute a lot during these meetings and while you were on the phone you didn't ask questions or share your ideas. What questions do you have about what I just shared?" This model has some good additions, such as asking the receiver if they have any questions, but is missing the alternative action that could replace the action that was observed.

Where the Models are Lacking

These are just a few of the many feedback models that can be used. Ultimately any model can be used to structure feedback, but it's about finding one that feels right for you. The challenge I've experienced is that each model has benefits but also has elements that are missing or unclear from the framework. As I've observed colleagues practicing giving feedback with several of these models, I noticed a few things.

First, people who are new to or uncomfortable giving feedback tend to stick strictly to the model, leading to a more rigid experience than a fluid discussion. In this case, while the model provides a framework that can create a more structured approach and alleviate some of the discomfort, it also can become a crutch to lean heavily on. This makes sense because when in an uncomfortable or stressful situation, we will hold on to what we know and where we can find structure.

The second finding from my observations is that the feedback tends to be one-directional, as the feedback giver rushes to hit all the steps on the model and be done with delivering the feedback. Because it's not typically a fun situation to provide constructive feedback to someone, the receiver just wants to get their thoughts out and then it tends to be like throwing a dart; quick, direct, and potentially off target. In these situations, even when the feedback giver pauses for input from the receiver, it tends to be more mechanical and tactical, because the model indicates to ask a question, rather than a true dialogue and co-creation of the next steps.

And lastly, from what I've seen, the feedback receiver tends to fill in the gaps and make assumptions around the behavior, and it's easy to make judgments about why the person behaved a certain way. Since we are wired to solve problems and avoid conflict, when we give feedback, we will tend to provide the solutions we see as the best options and circumvent a negative response from the other person by being direct and tactful rather than conversational. Alternately, the feedback may be "squishy" as we skirt around the real concern in an effort to not offend the other person or create conflict.

These key findings across various observations demonstrate that giving feedback is hard. Even when using a model or framework, it is usually an uncomfortable situation for both the giver and the receiver. That discomfort can lead to feedback that is ineffective, one-directional, judgmental, unclear, or rigid and formal.

Later in the book you'll learn a different approach to exchanging your perspective with someone so that you can share your observations and thoughts as well as provide space for them to do the same.

CHAPTER FOUR
Feedback Initiatives Within Organizations

Now that we know what feedback is and the underlying principles and models to use to structure our feedback, we should be an expert at giving feedback, right? Of course not, we'd need to apply and practice this skill to become an expert, but we should have at least a foundational understanding to set us up for success. In theory.

Organizational Feedback Efforts

For years companies have been spending time and money training employees at all levels on how to give and receive feedback. It's certainly an important skill to drive performance and improvement. Many organizations saturate this training, and yet it seems like many are still bad at it. Think about it, who loves getting feedback? Who loves giving feedback? There are exceptions, I'm sure, but most of us don't enjoy being on either end of feedback. We'll explore some of the neuroscience behind this later.

Despite it being a difficult skill to master and one that is often uncomfortable, even with some level of expertise and in the best situation, there is still a push to build a feedback culture. Employees are strongly encouraged to give each other and their managers feedback while managers are expected to do so for their team members. This push for feedback is nothing new. The question of how to get employees to improve has generated a lot of discussion and investigation since the middle of the last century.[8] To support this, employees and managers are trained, sometimes repeatedly, to get the concepts and preferred model(s) of the organization to stick. Despite anchoring to a specific feedback model, in research by *Strategy+Business* of over thirty models of feedback used within various organizations, these organizations indicated a lack of confidence that their model was effective at creating the lasting behavior change that was desired.[8]

Many organizations offer some form of feedback training to their people at all levels, and it's safe to say it's likely that a significant portion of the organization's population has received training on feedback. So, if most employees have been trained, why is this still so hard? Why are we still seeing a challenge for organizations to get it right and create a true feedback culture?

According to a McKinsey article, "Unlocking the true value of effective feedback conversations lies in equipping managers with the right tools to help them build their own capabilities."[9] We know we need to equip them with the right tools to be successful in delivering effective feedback. With the abundance of training taking place across the globe, why hasn't anyone unlocked the perfect toolkit and skilled their workforce up to effectively deliver feedback in a repeatable, sustainable way?

If we look at this from a conceptual lens, having a culture where feedback is shared frequently and effectively is one where we can help shrink blind spots and performance gaps. Colleagues at all levels embed feedback into regular discussions with the intention of improving the work to deliver better outcomes. Feedback is a key tool for organizations and personal relationships to create awareness. Feedback is here to stay.

Companies across the world include feedback as a core, required skill and continue to push training to their people. According to *Training* magazine, companies spend 16% of their overall budget to train their employees.[10] There are many challenges with the approach to focus on building skills around feedback and creating strict expectations to have productive, regular feedback conversations. To get to some of these challenges, a good question is what gets in the way of an effective feedback culture within an organization. The answer is many things. For one, if there is not a strong sense of psychological safety, feedback falls short.

And that's the best-case scenario, later we'll look at some of the impact of poorly delivered feedback or situations where perhaps the relationship or psychological safety is missing.

Feedback Loops

There are also a variety of formal feedback loops and employee listening platforms that organizations deploy to gain access to a wealth of information and insight. Programs like manager feedback surveys, employee engagement or pulse surveys and others are widely leveraged across a variety of industries. And we've all seen customer satisfaction surveys as consumers. The information gleaned from these vehicles are like gold to organizations looking to improve their operations and services to meet the needs of their customers and people. The challenge is that these feedback devices also rely on a certain level of psychological safety despite being presented as anonymous. From what I've experienced, as these platforms are implemented there is a sense of unease and suspicion from employees whether their feedback really is anonymous. People tend to anticipate negative consequences if they share their honest, constructive thoughts. More often than not, this mindset is rooted in one bad experience where they gave someone feedback and it was not well received or an occurrence where their current, or even a prior, manager has responded poorly to their feedback results. Thus, even if they have no basis for their current lack of trust, it tends to be deeply rooted in past experiences.

Another challenge with these feedback loops is that while they can provide insights and highlight issues within the organization, the solutions to those issues are typically created by people at a higher level of the organization who tend to be removed from the people experiencing the issues. Often without circling back to those who provided the feedback in the first place to see how this will help address what they are seeing. The result is a solution that doesn't fully address employee concerns. This is a better outcome than another typical response I've seen to feedback received in this manner, which is ignoring what has been shared. The impact of this is significant and generates the sentiment, "Why bother asking me if you don't care?" Over time, ignoring feedback conditions people to not respond or provide basic feedback that is not honest or valuable.

Lastly, formal feedback loops can lack a level of specificity needed to provide valuable insights. This requires the feedback receiver to fill in the gaps or feel as if the feedback is not actionable. Which then leads to it being ignored or dismissed resulting in the effect shared above of no longer wanting to provide feedback. Feedback is meant to be input and not necessarily a complete action list of everything that should be done to change or improve. Yet often that's how it's used so when it's not particularly specific or relevant it doesn't spark much self-reflection.

While these mechanisms for receiving more formal, broad-scale input from employees can be valuable and are an important part of building the feedback culture most organizations are striving for, it's clear there are innate barriers. I'm not suggesting eliminating these feedback loops, rather to create an awareness that for them to work well, a few things need to be true. First, there needs to be a high level of psychological safety and trust that the feedback will be taken with good intent. Second, the feedback should be reflected upon and generate ideas for solutions that are validated by those providing the feedback in some way. Lastly, regardless of how "actionable," specific, or relevant the feedback is to the receiver, it should be responded to in a way that makes the giver feels their thoughts have been acknowledged and encouraged to keep sharing their perspective.

Overall, it's clear that while information and insight can be gleaned using these mechanisms, which drives a focus for organizations to leverage listening platforms to get employee input, they should be viewed in the context of both the benefits and limitations that are common.

CHAPTER FIVE

Fundamental Feedback Flaws

Feedback can be a valuable and vital tool, and we've already explored some of the challenges with how to make this effective. Now let's dig in further to some more specific flaws that are inherent to feedback. Many of these are what will come to mind if you ask someone within an organization why building a feedback culture is so difficult and yet we've not quite cracked how to overcome these flaws in a scalable, impactful way.

The Six Flaws of Feedback

Fundamental Flaw #1: Threat Triggering (Our Brain on Feedback)

Perhaps the biggest flaw of feedback is that it triggers our fear response. Our brains are wired for survival as our top priority and therefore are built to protect us from threats, whether perceived or real. Its purpose is to "minimize danger and maximize reward." Even the statement, "I have some feedback for you" can create a physical response in our bodies where our heart rate increases, perhaps we begin sweating, as we obsess about what we did wrong. This interaction engages our amygdala which is the part of our brain responsible for our emotions and has a central role in how we respond to stressful situations and activates our flight, fight, or freeze response. The amygdala is a "cluster of almond-shaped cells located near the base of the brain. Everyone has two of these cell groups, one in each hemisphere (or side) of the brain"[11] that are a part of the brain's limbic system, an area of the brain responsible for our emotional and behavioral responses. Most people have heard of the flight or fight response, but the freeze component is a newer addition and just as valid a response to threats or danger.

When we hear that feedback is imminent, we reflect instantly on prior experiences, many of which were likely uncomfortable or upsetting. What we heard may have provided a perception of reality that is not aligned with our own and challenged us in some way. The threat present in feedback is not usually one that will truly harm us in a way that endangers our survival but as our threat centers have been highly attuned to new, more modern types of threats, our amygdala fires up as it prepares us to respond to avoid danger. We are then wired to make a quick decision on how to respond to this threat which doesn't engage our logic centers as the amygdala takes center stage shutting down the more logical areas within our brains.

Those viable responses are to fight, to flee, or to freeze. How that looks in a feedback situation may be much more subtle than a more life-threatening situation, but are present, nonetheless. You're probably familiar with flight or flight, and the more recent addition of freeze. Simply explained the fight response prepares us to engage physically with the danger to protect ourselves from harm. The flight, or flee, response is running away, or avoiding the danger. And lastly, the freeze response triggers us to stay put, hide, and don't react at all so as not to draw attention to ourselves. You can imagine that in a life-threatening situation being able to quickly react in one of these ways could be the difference between life or death.

Using the example when humans first walked the earth, imagine that you've encountered a sabretooth tiger. Your response may be to fight off the tiger to save yourself or your family, or you may immediately decide to run from the tiger and try to find a safe place, or you freeze because the tiger has yet to notice you and if you run it will chase you but if you don't move it may not see you as a threat or challenge and will leave you alone. In this scenario, you would want to be able to choose your course of action very quickly without a lot of contemplation to weigh endless options. Your brain is built to rapidly run through the neural pathways that you've created from prior experiences and make a split-second decision. It would flood your body with adrenaline so that you are primed to respond physically to ensure your survival. Your heart beats faster to pump blood and oxygen to your muscles, your eyesight gets sharper and even other senses become more heightened in preparation. You are now ready to react to the threat and hopefully live to see another day.

When it comes to feedback however, the threat that we perceive is usually not life-threatening or even something that can physically harm us. But as we do with many other "threats" in our lives, our brains treat it no differently than being in a potentially harmful situation. Logically it doesn't make sense to respond to feedback in the same way we would a bodily threat, but our frontal lobes, the logic centers in our brains, are dampened by the amygdala and thus not available to aid us in our response.

In an article by *Training Industry*, "According to David Rock, founder of NeuroLeadership Institute, we respond positively to constructive feedback (i.e., 'Here's what you did wrong') **only 1 out of 13 times**. The reason for is that our brain has five times as much real estate devoted to dealing with threats (e.g., negative feedback) as it does to dealing with rewards."[12] With all the real estate within our brains that is dedicated to ensuring our survival, it's no wonder we are on high alert, constantly surveying our environment for danger.

Let's use the example from above to see how this could play out: John was looking at his phone during the team meeting and he receives the feedback that it is disruptive and not considerate of other team members, and he shouldn't be distracted during these discussions. Based on what we learned above, we could expect to see one of three responses:

- **Fight**: John disagrees, responding with anger and frustration, or even defensively explaining why what he did was right.
- **Flee/Flight**: John walks out of the room, avoiding the conversation, or completely ignores what he heard.
- **Freeze**: John completely shuts down, withdrawing from the conversation and stares silently, or he may even smile and nod without really processing.

While we can't be sure of which response will be triggered in John, it is unlikely he was able to focus on the message, process what he heard, and feel personally committed to changing his behaviors. He may apply what he was told to do to resolve this situation without autonomy or ownership of the solution likely as a way to avoid future confrontation or stay out of trouble.

Who are we to argue with neuroscience? Instead of working against how our brains are wired there are many schools of thought around how to improve the feedback experience that incorporate what we know about neuroscience and its role in how we respond to feedback. We will explore some of these a bit later.

Fundamental Flaw #2: Monologue vs. Dialogue

Have you ever received feedback that was just a monologue from the other person? They essentially just have a speech prepared in which they tell you what you did and how that created a negative consequence and what to do next time. There may be some conversation as you get started or perhaps at the end, but it feels mostly one-sided. It's like you're in the audience watching Act 3, Scene 2 of Shakespeare's Henry VIII: Part 3 which is the longest soliloquy in his works.[13] Or watching the closing argument given by Orson Welles' character, Jonathan Wilk in Compulsion, noted as the longest true monologue in film history at fifteen minutes, according to Filmsite.org.[14]

Orson Welles in a courtroom [15]

This experience is one where the feedback giver downloads their perspective to the feedback receiver. This happens for a few reasons. First, there could be a level of discomfort in having the discussion on the part of the feedback giver which results in a rush to deliver the feedback and move on. Also, if you recall from the earlier chapter on principles, while the intent is to have a discussion where there is an exchange of dialogue, in reality the discomfort plays a role as does an over-reliance on a structured feedback model that provides that bit of comfort and control.

Another reason feedback tends to be one-sided is the nature of feedback itself. You'll recall the definition of feedback is a tool used by professional organizations, educational institutions, and personal relationships to provide information about another's behavior or actions with the intent of changing, stopping, or improving that behavior or action. So, we approach it as providing input or information which then tends to be one-directional.

Being on the receiving end of a one-directional feedback session leaves one feeling discouraged. As professionals, while we benefit from being redirected, when we don't have the opportunity to contribute to the discussion it becomes a reprimand, perceived as a scolding which stirs emotions of frustration, embarrassment, and anger. Rather than address how we approach these discussions we try to teach people to stay calm and don't get angry, but of course we're not wired that way as was outlined in the first flaw. With a lot of practice, we can get better at receiving feedback but why not also adjust our approach to align better to how we're wired and how we perceive one-way input?

I propose that rather than a monologue of monotony shift toward dialogues of discovery. Seek to understand each other's perspectives and make it a discussion where you listen to each other and acknowledge that each person has a valid perspective to share. Approach the conversation with curiosity, empathy, and interest in what the other person wants to share as much as what you need to say.

Fundamental Flaw #3: Know-Best Bias

When we give feedback, we tend to assume that we know better and have more expertise and experience to give to another person to provide insights that they don't have. While this may be the case, it's not always true. I call this expertise bias or "know-best bias." There is a bit of egocentric bias contributing to this as well, where we rely too significantly on our own perspective and have a higher opinion of ourselves than may be based on reality. This is a cognitive bias also results in us underestimating how different other people's viewpoint is from their own or to ignore other people's viewpoint entirely.[16]

We believe that our input is valuable, needed, and right. This is based on us experiencing similar situations or receiving similar advice in the past and perceiving a degree of success with the outcome. We believe we know not only what the right solution or behavior is, we also believe that we know exactly why someone acted in a certain way and that it is not the right way to behave.

This trap is an easy one to fall into especially as we grow in our own careers and accumulate experiences and success. We become wise and want to extend that wisdom to others to help them be successful too. We want them to benefit from our experiences and the challenges that we've overcome. So, with good intentions, we give them our feedback, assuming that we know best and can help someone else as a result of that knowledge.

What this doesn't consider is that we're all different and even similar situations can be nuanced. Sharing our perspective and what we see as opportunity to improve or shift behaviors can be extremely valuable, but it's not often that we stop to ask ourselves, do I have all the information I need to make a judgment, do I really understand what's going on here? So, in this case, simply approaching it with the mindset of "this is how I see it" and engaging in a dialogue to hear how the other person sees it could go a long way to breaking down this bias.

Next time you need to provide feedback instead of assuming you know best, ask yourself what you really know and what do you need to understand from the other person to enable you to provide a more meaningful perspective to them or even challenge your own perspective. And remember the more experience and knowledge we gain the easier it is to fall into this trap. This knowledge is extremely valuable but rather assuming it supersedes the knowledge of the other person, it's helpful to pause before sharing this as an ultimate truth.

Fundamental Flaw #4: Perpetual Dependency Loop

You are probably familiar with the "teach a person to fish" proverb. In case you're not, it goes something like this: if you fish for a person, they will never be able to feed themselves without you, but if you teach them how to fish, they will never go hungry again. The moral of the story is to help people learn how to do something for themselves instead of doing it for them.

I mention this because it relates to how we typically are "fishing for someone" rather than "teaching them to fish" when we give feedback in traditional ways. When we give someone a "fish" they keep coming back to us for more fish rather than being able to fish for themselves. This creates a dependency on someone else to provide the sustenance that is needed to survive. It is quite similar with feedback, when we provide feedback without engaging the other person in the solutioning we are providing them answers and thus create a dependency upon us for those answers in the future.

I call this the perpetual dependency loop. The more we provide the answer or tell someone how to do something the more people will rely on you to continue to do just that. This is rooted in how our brains create new neural pathways. A neural pathway is a series of connected nerves along which an electrical impulse is transmitted. These pathways send signals from one area of our brain to another. When we learn something, we program that into our brain so that we can easily access that learning and information more rapidly in the future. Think of this as paving a road so that the traffic can flow more freely from point A to point B. New neural pathways are created when we encounter something new, and our brain tests this new information against what we already know. And as we build these pathways our brain will follow those same pathways when we encounter that same, or similar, thing or situation again allowing us to more quickly identify what it is and what response is needed, if any. The more we learn and repeat the same behaviors the stronger that pathway gets, while the opposite is true, if we don't practice that skill or behavior our brain "disconnects" the unused pathway.[17]

Perhaps even more interestingly, if we have an emotional response to that new situation, thing, or information, such as fear, the neural pathway that forms will associate that emotion with a similar situation, thing, or information going forward. In this case, the best approach would be to try to create new associations and provide new information for which to create a new pathway.[17] This helps us understand a couple of things. First, we can better understand how a negative feedback episode creates an association of the emotion we experienced or negativity with feedback in general and thus prepares us for that when we encounter feedback in the future. Second, people will tap into the neural pathways they've built and if we can help them test those patterns of thinking we can help them reframe experiences and even potentially build new pathways that allow them to better navigate similar experiences going forward. Consider this as we offer advice, because it may not allow people to form new thinking patterns for themselves, thus expanding their own neural pathways because we've given them an answer that doesn't require deep thought on their part.

Our desire to help others and share our experiences in the form of advice drives us to offer solutions to other people. We want to help them improve or get unstuck, or, even to stop doing something that adversely impacts us in some way. Another driver for providing an alternative behavior for someone is that it feels good for us to share our knowledge and we enjoy giving advice. It feels good to be the one who has the answers and knows what to do to be successful. In this way there is perceived benefit from creating the perpetual dependency loop because others come to us for our wisdom.

However, providing feedback that tells someone exactly how to behave denies an opportunity for them to think for themselves and try to figure out their way forward on their own, and doesn't help them in the long run. Nor does it help us.

When a perpetual dependency loop is created, the feedback receiver will continue to rely on the feedback giver for advice. The outcome of feedback should be to spark self-reflection so that over time less feedback is needed to help close the person's blind spot because it has gotten smaller. Traditional feedback limits this spark by telling someone what they did "wrong" and what to do instead. And rather than seeking to shrink someone's blind spot to reduce their dependency upon feedback, traditional feedback encourages continued reliance upon us and thus our need to continue to spend time and energy providing feedback to that person. Later, we will explore some ways to bypass this and avoid creating a perpetual dependency loop.

Fundamental Flaw #5: Looking Backward

By its nature, feedback is sharing information about something that happened in the past, however long ago that past may be. I see two primary flaws within this principle that present challenges to delivering successful feedback.

First, if you recall the principles outlined earlier, timeliness is key, but how we define what "timely" means can be vague or inconsistent. Ideally, the feedback would be delivered as soon as possible after the behavior or situation was observed so that it is relatively fresh in everyone's mind. The longer the feedback is held after the behavior occurred, the more unclear our recollections become as we try to think back further and further.

Think, for a moment, have you ever received feedback that felt stale because so much time had passed that you could not recall the details or even the specific example raised? How did it feel in that moment? I suspect feelings of confusion, frustration, and even anger were present. You may have asked clarifying questions to jog your memory and found that either the feedback giver's memory was almost equally unclear or that they recalled specifics that you couldn't. In this situation, it is difficult to process and absorb the feedback in a way that allows you to own what you heard and how you will move forward.

Second, regardless of how much time elapses between when the behavior was observed and when the feedback is given, feedback tends to emphasize what happened in the past with limited attention on what should happen moving forward. If done well, equal time should be spent on discussing the past as well as planning for the future, but most feedback tends to be inclined toward looking backward.

What time is spent on discussing the future usually summarizes the expected behavior from the perspective of the feedback giver. The alternative behavior is suggested as "do this instead." Often not enough importance is given to gaining alignment on the goal and the future behaviors as agreed to by the feedback receiver.

In summary, if feedback isn't shared within a reasonable period of time, it becomes stale and less likely that the feedback receiver will connect to the situation or feedback that addresses it. Coupled with an emphasis on the past rather than the future, the flaw of looking backward, presents challenges to delivering effective feedback.

Fundamental Flaw #6: Rapport Required

One of the keys to successful feedback is having some trusting relationship from which to operate from. Without that rapport, the feedback may carry less weight or value, depending on the situation. For example, feedback from a trusted manager or team member may be given more significance than feedback received from someone we don't know or don't like or trust very much.

Reflect for a moment on a time where you received feedback from someone you didn't like or respect. How much weight did you give that feedback initially? Perhaps you spent more time discussing the feedback with trusted colleagues or friends and it became more valid for you. It takes a certain level of maturity and self-reflection to be able to pause and ask yourself those hard questions about what you're hearing. It's much easier to discount or ignore feedback from someone who you don't have a relationship with.

Throughout my career I have received plenty of feedback from people I didn't respect or like. One such example was from a manager who micromanaged the team and pushed her own way of managing onto others. At the time, I was managing a team and her style of management was very different from my own. Additionally, she was quick to take the credit for the impact the team created without sharing that with us, which I didn't appreciate. During one of our performance reviews, she gave me feedback that I needed to spend "more time with the team." From my perspective, there were a lot of issues with this feedback. The comment was vague, I wasn't clear what "more time" meant. There were not any specific examples of where I spent "less time" with my team. The impact of not spending enough time with my team was also unspecified. This all left me confused and trying to understand what I was doing and how my team was negatively impacted as a result.

I asked clarifying questions and didn't get any additional information of substance to help me process the feedback. The response was that she didn't see me stop by their desks as much as she would like. My initial instinct was to discard what she told me because 1) I didn't respect her or her leadership and 2) I didn't agree with her because she hadn't shared any information that could help me better understand the feedback. If we had a better relationship, it would have been easier for me to talk through it and even take what she shared as being with good intent because she cared about me and my career. In this case, I wanted to just ignore it because feedback directly from my team had been positive around this topic.

Despite the relationship being strained, I did go back and reflect upon this further not because I cared about her but because I cared about the team. In this situation, it was my ability to connect to the rapport with my team which inspired me to pause and dig into what I heard, despite not agreeing to it and having poor rapport with the feedback giver. Earlier in my career, I would have easily discarded the feedback, but as I matured in my development, I was able to look beyond who gave me the feedback to concentrate instead on determining whether what she said had merit.

However, to be able to do this requires a certain level of emotional intelligence as well as growth mindset on the part of the feedback receiver, which isn't always present. The theory of emotional intelligence was introduced in the 1990s by Peter Salovey and John D. Mayer, further developed by Daniel Goleman. You may be familiar with EQ which this is also known as. Emotional intelligence is "the ability to identify and manage one's own emotions, as well as the emotions of others."[18] Recall that the feedback experience is one that can provoke a variety of emotions. Emotional intelligence enables people to "harness those emotions and apply them to tasks like thinking and problem solving."[18]

According to her studies on human motivation, psychologist Carol S. Dweck, PhD, describes growth mindset as a belief that intelligence can be developed. This mindset leads one to learn from criticism, persist in the face of setbacks, and embrace challenges. The benefit of having emotional intelligence, being able to leverage one's emotional energy for productive outcomes, and growth mindset, the ability to approach criticism and challenge as an opportunity to learn and grow, is significant when it comes to receiving feedback in a positive way. In fact, much of how we teach people to get better at receiving feedback is based on these concepts. These become even more important in the absence of a trusting relationship between the feedback giver and receiver.[19]

Another way to look at this is to consider the relationship as being a connection in which the success of the feedback receiver is somehow dependent upon the feedback giver. When this is a situation such as a manager and their team member, the team member is more likely to heed the feedback from their manager simply because if they don't it may affect their performance and ultimately their job. In this case, the feedback is not as powerful as if it is given by a manager or person where there is strong rapport and thus is deeply trusted and taken in. The difference here is compliance vs. commitment. We may comply with what a person in a position of power over us tells us, but we will more likely commit to the alternative actions from feedback we heard when we have a trusting relationship with that person.

In our typical feedback situations at work, either a level of rapport is needed or a high level of emotional intelligence and growth mindset on the part of the feedback receiver must be present for the feedback to be effectively absorbed and acted upon. If the relationship is one where trust is absent, but power is present, we may still take the feedback and comply to stay out of trouble or avoid a negative impact to our career rather than fully committing to changing the behaviors.

Fundamentally Flawed... A Summary

There are several principles we discussed earlier that act as guidelines for effective feedback. However, the reality gap exists between the principle in *theory* and the principle in *application*. Even if applied with the best intent, there are fundamental flaws that exist within traditional feedback.

In this chapter we learned about these flaws. Feedback triggers our innate threat response, while we can condition ourselves to lessen the threat response, it is built into our DNA and wired in our brains. The monologic nature of feedback can feel one-sided and when the feedback giver embodies an "I know best" attitude, providing their solution for alternative behaviors, there isn't much personal connection or commitment to the go-forward actions by the feedback receiver because they weren't involved in the discussion or solutioning. By providing advice, a perpetual dependency loop is created, where the feedback receiver relies on the feedback giver to continue to give their advice. Focused on the past more than on the future, and waiting too long to provide the feedback, makes it challenging to connect to the feedback and focus on go-forward goals. Lastly, without strong rapport, the feedback can be discarded unless the feedback giver has well-developed emotional intelligence and growth mindset.

In chapter eight, we will examine how to overcome or bypass these flaws to enable a productive conversation where perspectives can be shared and heard.

CHAPTER SIX

The Lasting Impact Feedback Can Have

In this chapter we will explore the impact that feedback can have on people, both how they may unrealistically adapt their behaviors as a result and how they create mechanisms to deal with, or avoid, feedback situations in the future. This can be a result of even well-intentioned feedback almost as much as poorly delivered or hyper-critical feedback.

A Gift

We're told that feedback is a gift. That we should openly welcome feedback and be grateful for it. It's a great mentality to have and certainly is part of having a growth mindset, as outlined earlier. If we remove the emotion and address the flaws inherent to feedback, we can view feedback simply as information for us to process and apply in a way that that helps us improve and grow. In this way, it can be a gift, it can help us expose our blind spots and realize where we need to improve. However, have you ever received a gift you didn't like? Have you ever returned a gift because it didn't fit you or your personality? As we say with gifts, it's the thought that counts. We can still be grateful for the gift even if we want to return or exchange it for something that better fits us.

"Feedback is a gift" is a perfect metaphor in this way as it is the thought that matters and for the feedback receiver to determine whether the feedback "fits" or should be "returned." As you recall that we should try to consider feedback simply as information for us to process, it would seem that this should be relatively easy for us to do. Yet when we bring in the neuroscience to understand how our brain responds to this information, it all gets a bit complicated. Regardless of whether the feedback experience is a good one or not, the result can be an impact that lasts a lifetime.

Feedback Fallout

There are many positive, lasting impacts of feedback, several which have already been highlighted; feedback can broaden your perspective, shrink your blind spots, and help you develop and grow. These positive outcomes can be a product of both positive and negative feedback experiences. However, as discussed earlier, a negative feedback experience resulting in a positive outcome strongly relies on the presence of growth mindset and emotional intelligence. Even with these present there tends to be fallout from the feedback that leaves a scar that never fully heals.

My experience coaching and mentoring a diverse group of colleagues and friends has left me with insights into how those feedback experiences become deeply buried within the subconscious producing behaviors and mindsets that ultimately do not serve them well. They absorb another's opinion and try to force fit it into how they behave. The consequences end up being striving for "always" or "never" behaviors when rarely in life do those adverbs apply. I will share some of those experiences with you to illustrate the short-term and lasting fallout feedback can have.

I have worked with both men and women and will highlight the disproportionate impact I have seen on women, particularly damaging their confidence and sense of self-worth and inner strength. In these examples names have been changed but the details are unaltered. The exception to this is the first example, my son, Aiden.

Case Study #1: Aiden

When my son was eleven years old, he received some feedback. To set some context, he received his feedback in an educational setting the year after he returned to in-person schooling in the 2021-2022 school year during the COVID-19 pandemic. Anyone who experienced schooling during the pandemic knows what a challenging time it was as educators and students needed to pivot quickly and the level of ambiguity and fear was high. On top of all of this, Aiden wrestled with a history of anxiety and Attention-Deficit/Hyperactivity Disorder (ADHD). So, even in the best of circumstances, school could be challenging for him.

Aiden joined band in fifth grade and was eager to learn and explore creativity through music. This was exciting to us as traditional instruction methods of memorization tended to be difficult for Aiden. We knew memorizing notes and chords would be part of his learning but hoped that this would also ultimately be an outlet for his creativity and curiosity. Despite

The Lasting Impact Feedback Can Have

his initial excitement, getting him to practice and focus was an obstacle.

He quickly became frustrated with the mechanics and intricacies of playing an instrument. We worked together to break it down into smaller pieces and help him work through those frustrations. Without musical aptitude myself, I did the best I could without being able to lend my own expertise. But together, we figured it out.

Then it was time for his first assignment, submitting a video of him playing a particular piece — one that I had never heard of, so we leveraged the power of the internet to watch videos and listen to the song, over and over, to get a sense of how it should sound. Aiden practiced, and practiced, and practiced some more. He worked through a rollercoaster of emotions and persisted despite wanting to give up several times. He must have played that song 100 times.

He submitted his video, and we knew it wasn't perfect. We encouraged him to reflect and decide whether this was his best version to submit. He felt like he was ready. We knew there was room for improvement but also acknowledged all his hard work to get to this point. With pride he uploaded his video and pressed "submit."

Two days later he received a voice message from an instructor. We listened to it together. As the message played, I watch the smile disappear from Aiden's face and the light fade from his eyes. It went something like this; "Aiden, what song were you playing? Did you listen to the song you were supposed to play? I couldn't even tell what you were playing." The message continued and provided some decent feedback and advice. But that message was completely lost because of those first words. Words that conveyed failure and sentiments like "you messed up," "that was awful," and "you have no idea what you are doing."

Clearly, this is an example of good feedback gone wrong. The band instructor let their own frustration out in those first few statements rather than setting them aside, focusing on the goal and student, and helping him move forward. They could have omitted those words and had a completely different impact on my son. They could have rephrased those words and had a completely different impact on my son. They could have been more empathetic understanding Aiden as an individual and recognizing how picking up an instrument for the first time could be challenging for him. They could have encouraged him to try again providing insight to help him improve. They should have done all of that. Instead, Aiden finished out the year in band and decided to quit because he "couldn't do it." I wonder who put that idea into his head?

In fact, as the year went on the instructor took a more Aiden-centered approach. They took the time to talk to him and understand what was particularly challenging and came up with ideas on how to teach to Aiden's strengths and ways of learning. It became clear the instructor really cared about helping Aiden and inspiring a passion for music within him. Unfortunately, by that time it was too late, from Aiden's perspective he wasn't smart enough or good enough to continue to play an instrument. As a parent, seeing your child feel deflated breaks your heart. As a leader, I reflected upon all of the similar experiences I've encountered in the workplace.

The lesson in this is that when we give feedback it is easy to allow our own frustrations and emotions guide our message and intent. With our "know-best bias," it's easy as the "expert" to be disappointed, or even annoyed, that someone is not performing at your expected level of excellence. And lastly, that even if you put in the work to come back from projecting those frustrations and disappointments on someone else, the damage could already be done.

Perhaps acknowledging that frustration and even apologizing could go a long way to getting back on track, but in our case the decision had already been made to quit.

Case Study #2: Joan

Joan is a smart, talented woman. She also is a more introspective and soft-spoken person. She is not quick to share her ideas first and does not use a loud voice to get her point across or influence others. Her role as an Assistant Vice President required her to be able to articulate strategic messages and influence leaders in the organization.

As many other women do, Joan received the feedback that she needs to make sure her voice is heard in meetings. She needed to "challenge more" and readily push people to the outcome she wanted to drive. She was told by her manager that this is crucial for her as a female leader to not be left behind and to grow in her career.

Theoretically, the message isn't necessarily wrong. As a leader who is looking to expand her career, she will need to influence and challenge others to get to impactful outcomes. But rather than agree on what her goals as a leader are and help her find her own way to do that, she was told if she wanted to move up in the organization she needed to speak louder, more often, and question people as a form of influence.

Shortly after receiving this feedback Joan showed up in meetings much differently than she had before. Where she was typically quiet in certain meetings, only speaking up when she had something of value to add, she started speaking up more. Rather than contributing her own thoughts she would reiterate what someone else said to be sure her voice was heard. She started challenging asking the same questions: "What are you trying to accomplish?" or "What is the problem you are trying to solve?" These questions are great, when applied at the right time and with the right context. But these became her go to way to push her colleagues and would result in derailing the discussion rather than moving it forward in a way that was thoughtful and impactful.

In a word it was awkward. It was not authentic to her personality or leadership style. It felt forced and was a perfect example of the "always" application. She took the feedback and made sure that she "always" spoke up during the conversation or meeting, regardless of whether she actually contributed to it or not. She "always" asked questions of her colleagues, regardless of whether it made sense to do so. This awkwardness was felt by Joan and her colleagues. Rather than creating the positive results she desired, she found she was having the opposite effect.

Joan unconditionally followed the advice within the feedback she received, adopting behaviors that were inconsistent with who she is. When we talked, I asked Joan the questions she asked of others, what she was trying to accomplish and what problem was she trying to solve. In our discussion we created space for her to consider what kind of leader she wanted to be. How would she use her strengths to influence others? How would she use her voice or her talents to create the impact she envisioned? She discovered an authentic way for her to create the impact she desired allowing her to grow in her career as a vice president. In a time when authentic leadership is valuable, she unlocked the authentic leader within and found her own way to accomplish her goals.

Case Study #3: Michelle

Michelle was navigating her career options when we met. She was eager to grow and create bigger impact and take on more challenging roles. Despite being bright and a strong performer she couldn't quite figure out how to move forward in her career. Couldn't understand what was holding her back.

Michelle was fortunate to have a manager and leader who wanted her to succeed. They helped her realize that she was putting a lot of effort into perfecting her work product and while quality was important, she needed to find balance with delivering with speed. She came to realize that her pursuit of perfection was causing her to over work and over think things. It was slowing her down and inhibiting her ability to quickly iterate, get input from others, and adjust from there. Her goal was to deliver a perfect work product, despite whether that level of quality was needed or not.

Michelle came to me for coaching with the goal to identify techniques to find the balance between speed and quality and eventually take on more responsibility so she could demonstrate her ability to tackle more challenging roles. Through her discussions with her manager, she realized that when she was spending so much time on getting everything right, she didn't have time to take on and learn new responsibilities.

When we explored what was getting in her way, she expressed a fear of failure. Most people don't enjoy failing and at one time or another probably allow that fear to spark hesitancy and even avoidance. This fear happens to many of us. A 2015 survey by Linkagoal "found that a fear of failure plagued 31% of respondents, a larger percent than those that feared spiders (30%), being home alone (9%) or even the paranormal (15%)."[20] However, when this fear drives a need for constant perfection it is like an anchor wrapped around us, dragging us further and further down.

As part of our discussions, we sought to free Michelle from that anchor and let go of the mantra "what if I fail?" She shared a story with me that she felt like was at the root of her fear. Earlier in her career she received some feedback that stuck with her. She was presenting in a meeting and was nervous despite being well prepared. She felt that the meeting went well and while there were some questions that she didn't have the answer to, she knew that she could go get that information and circle back with the audience.

Her manager provided her with some feedback after the meeting. He told her that when she presents, she must be ready for any question that may come up and be able to answer it on the spot. He explained that the impact of not knowing the answer is that she looks unprepared and unknowledgeable. His expectations of her were to anticipate these questions and have responses ready to address them.

He never asked her how she felt about the meeting or what she thought went well or that could have gone better. He never asked for her response to his own perception of the meeting. From her perspective, her manager just told her that she had made a mistake and if she wanted to be in his shoes someday, she needed to have all the answers all the time. She explained her approach and that she did indeed prepare for the meeting and pointed out that she did respond well to several of the questions. This didn't go over very well, and she left the discussion thinking, *I'll never make a mistake again.*

When she shared this with me it was clear the impact this one piece of feedback had on her. I asked, "How realistic is it to have a goal of never making a mistake again?" and we talked about how even the greatest of the greats, those who train their whole lives in a particular sport or area of expertise, make mistakes. They miss shots, they strike out, they trip and fall. But they get back up, they learn, and they keep going. We talked about whether perfection is attainable and if so at what cost.

This feedback was one moment over a decade ago, yet it persisted. It continued to gnaw at her confidence and resulted in her overworking because she had to make sure everything that she produced was 100% correct 100% of the time. That she knew all the answers and anticipated all the questions. She had vowed to never make a mistake again.

I asked her to complete this statement, "Practice makes..." and without hesitation she filled in with "perfect." She felt that if she just spent enough time practicing and checking, and double-checking, that she could attain perfection. And maybe she could. Sometimes. And in those situations when perfection was achieved, what else didn't get done. Where else could that time have been spent. We talked about when perfection was really needed and when was good enough good enough. I shared that my kids were learning a different saying, if I say to them "Practice makes . . . ," they say "Progress." And so, rather than striving for perfect perfection, she thought about how she could focus on progress.

Our conversations helped her to identify the optimal level of quality needed and how to own her knowledge and expertise without knowing everything. She had to learn to move past one piece of feedback and find her way forward. Feedback that was intended to help her ended up manifesting into an obstacle. It fueled her fears and thus an expedition for perfection that was always just out of reach. This feedback fallout had plagued Michelle for over a decade, always lurking. She was so afraid to make a mistake that she was burning herself out, working more hours than was needed to deliver the work and creating a fierce independence and reluctance to ask for help or admit when she didn't know something.

Michelle's example demonstrates how easily even well-intentioned feedback can morph into a negative, lasting experience that triggers irrational fears and unrealistic expectations.

Case Study #4: Sean

Sean received some accusatory feedback early in his career from a colleague who was more senior than him in the organization. Sean was supporting a leader who was new to the group and looking to bring in their own ideas and ways of working. It's not uncommon for new leaders to want to make changes as soon as possible to "make their mark" on the organization, assert their influence, and establish themselves in their role. But when this is done without

The Lasting Impact Feedback Can Have

thoughtful consideration and understanding of the current state and where improvement would be beneficial, this can become change for the sake of change, which is usually not well received by employees.

Sean sought to provide counsel and insight to this new leader to help direct their approach. Early in their relationship there was tension and misalignment, particularly of the leader's expectation of Sean's role. The leader did not want guidance but rather expected Sean to take specific direction and execute on their wishes.

A few weeks into the relationship, they got into a disagreement about whether to hire for a role that had been eliminated as part of a reorganizational effort prior to the new leader joining. Sean pushed back, attempting to share the background and provide information for the leader to consider. The leader did not appreciate being challenged and the two argued over what to do. During this argument, Sean provided incorrect information about the hiring process for the role in question. Clearly, the discussion was driven by emotions on both sides and the meeting concluded without clear resolution.

Later that day, the leader scheduled a meeting with Sean's manager and their manager, the Vice President of the organization. The leader shared that what they were told by Sean was incorrect, rather than approaching Sean directly first and giving him the opportunity to address the issue and mistake. After this meeting, the leader reached out to Sean and accused him of lying.

As you can imagine, Sean was devastated by receiving this type of feedback. This leader assumed bad intent by Sean rather than providing factual feedback that the information

Sean provided was incorrect and asking him what happened. Not only was ill intent assumed, but also the leader went above Sean to his manager and his manager's manager to complain and provide the feedback.

The relationship between Sean and this leader was never the same after, there was a complete lack of trust between the two. It took Sean several weeks to rebuild his confidence and move past the feedback interaction and the way in which it was approached. Reeling from the feedback caused Sean to over-correct his behaviors so much that he refrained from challenging leaders or providing a different opinion from theirs, even in situations he knew they were making a mistake.

It took support from a peer to help Sean navigate the experience and process the feedback. Together, they acknowledged that the way the feedback was delivered was out of line but focused on what facts could be taken from the feedback for Sean to focus on. This helped him move past his emotions and begin to reflect on what adjustments he could make in his approach rather than course correcting so severely that he was unable to effectively challenge leaders' thoughts and behaviors, which was a key part of his role.

Sean's example is a good one because it exemplifies what happens when feedback principle #7 is not followed. You'll recall that this principle is to remain objective in the feedback and to refrain from making assumptions or judgments. In this case, the leader assumed that Sean intentionally lied about the hiring process rather than considering that potentially he had made a mistake. There are several other principles that were broken in this example as well as flaws highlighted, but this one stands out to me the most.

That leader's value judgment and assumption deeply hurt Sean and rattled his confidence in a way that could have prevented him from providing valuable input and information to leaders in the future. He was fortunate to have a team member to process this information with that allowed him to step back out of the emotion and approach the situation, as painful and embarrassing as it had been, with a more logical lens. In this way, he was able to make minor adjustments rather than to abstain from providing his thoughts all together or spending so much time making sure he was right that he couldn't provide information timely.

Case Study #5: Liz

Liz's story is a bit different and is a great illustration of the mechanisms used within organizations to capture feedback that were mentioned earlier. Liz's organization was experiencing massive changes as her company was merged with another. This resulted in a lot of new people coming together and two distinct cultures clashing a bit as they tried to figure out their way forward.

As she experienced this transition, including a change in management structure, she was eager to accelerate her adjustment to her new manager and team members. To help her navigate this she asked her manager for feedback to understand how she was doing. Her manager suggested a 360 survey for her to be able to capture input from a group of selected team members and stakeholders. For those not familiar, a 360 survey, or 360-degree survey, allows an individual to obtain anonymous feedback from colleagues at all levels, their manager, their direct reports, and their peers.

The individual also provides a self-assessment for which to compare the perspectives from the other groups to.

This can be an effective tool to create self-awareness. However, there are some challenges inherent to this method, one is that the number of respondents is limited to allow for an optimal scope of perspectives that can be effectively processed without being overwhelming, which tends to be somewhere between five and seven. Another is that typically the feedback receiver selects who they want to receive feedback from. As a result, a manager may be required to select only some of their team members to receive input from rather than the whole team. Even if someone is not a manager, when selecting whom to receive feedback from, there is a bias toward those who will provide more positive perspectives than those who will share critiques.

In the case of Liz, she selected a handful of people to get input from and her manager added to that list. The 360-survey asked for input from those team members selected around what was working well, what could be improved, and what are some words that come to mind when they think of Liz. Seems straightforward enough, right?

Unfortunately, this is an example demonstrating how what is logical in theory can lead to unintended consequences, falling short in application. When Liz received her 360 results, she found herself drawn to the words that her colleagues had shared, words that provided no context. Some of these words were very positive and Liz could reflect on examples where that description showed up in her interactions with the team. Other words, like "scattered" and "unreliable" sparked further reflection on Liz's part. As she wracked her brain trying to come up with examples where she missed deadlines or let her team down, she came up empty.

Unable to connect to specific examples and without additional context Liz was left to fill in the blanks for herself. She found herself stuck in the "emotionally crushing vibe" she got from the 360. She took on the feedback and looked to find a path forward where she wouldn't let anyone down or be considered unreliable. She became bitter and robotic. In doing so she misplaced those qualities that made her great and stand out positively to her colleagues of being warm and friendly.

As Liz processed all of this, she was fortunate to have a friend who coached her how to effectively deal with the emotion and frustration she experienced. She worked to reframe and own the words to make them work for her, instead of against her, as a motivating factor. She spoke to her manager, sharing her experience and that the words without context weren't constructive. Her manager's response was for her to consider how it may be constructive as over time those words shift to more positive perspectives of the team. What was unclear was the harm the feedback had caused for Liz and the work she had to put in to navigate a way forward that allowed her to embrace and adapt to what she heard while retaining the best parts of herself.

Fortunately, Liz has come through this experience and has gotten to a better place, though not without bearing some significant feedback scars. She still has work to do to find a way forward that feels right for her. At times she felt like giving up and unsure of her footing and her own strengths and abilities. Feedback can help bring awareness to blind spots and broaden our own perspectives by understanding those of others. When we consider what we know about our brain's response to feedback, it's no surprise how the feedback Liz received was perceived as a threat by her brain and thus prepared her to respond accordingly.

Disproportionate Impact on Women

Throughout years of managing and coaching I have heard examples just like these. From men and from women. However, while both genders have similar experiences the impression left on women is drastically different.

In my experience, women tend to hold onto the feedback in a way that can erode self-esteem and confidence. While I have seen this happen with some men as well, it is less common in those I've worked with over the years. There has been some research supporting this as well. Several studies are highlighted in an article from Quartz at Work provide evidence that as women "other people's negative opinions can have an outsize effect on our self-image, deterring us from pursuing goals and new opportunities." The article goes on to argue that this may not always be a disadvantage as women are better at internalizing and reflecting upon feedback in a way that allows us to better understand other's perceptions as well as our reality.[21]

My own experience reflects the studies outlined in the article. Women tend to adjust their view of their performance more often and more severely upon receiving critical feedback than men do.[22] As noted, while this may not necessarily become a hindrance to woman there are clear implications to self-assurance as we accept other's perspectives as reality. This may evolve to become a strength as women are able to take in other perspectives and adjust their behavior to become more successful, but at what expense? Are they losing some of what makes them unique and able to bring diversity of thought and action?

Consider it this way. Women receive feedback in various ways, as illustrated above. Think of each piece of feedback as a piece of clothing. Clothing that doesn't quite fit our body or our style. So, we take this clothing, as is, and put it on, it feels uncomfortable, but we know we're supposed to accept the "gift" and make it ours. First, we get an itchy sweater, then we layer on top a jacket that is just a little too small, next we throw a scarf on that is not ours at all and doesn't work with our style. Top it off with a hat that's just too big and keeps falling over our eyes. While we should take these items and tailor them to ourselves, wear what works only when it works, and even discard or donate what doesn't work for us, women typically just take it all on until we're eventually buried underneath all the ill-fitting layers, suppressing our natural strengths.

One other phenomenon that contributes to this is that sometimes women are receiving feedback from men, who advise them to behave more like them, or by women, who have had to behave more like men to be successful and thus pass that advice on to other women. Feedback such as this results in conditioning of women to lead or behave like men rather than leveraging those feminine qualities to our advantage.

An example of this was in feedback I received as part of a high-potential leadership program. The intention of the program was to accelerate talent by providing an opportunity to practice being in difficult situations that senior leaders encounter frequently. We started by getting very limited information and time to prepare to be a senior executive at an imaginary company, and were given a brief bio and financials for that company. We then participated in mock situations, an executive leadership team meeting, a difficult customer discussion, a challenging employee situation, and a strategy presentation to the CEO. Throughout the experience we were videotaped and examined by both external and internal observers who were then tasked with sharing their observations and feedback.

A senior leader provided feedback to me; he told me I needed to be more assertive in my leadership. His example was during the mock leadership team meeting that I had taken charge to grab the marker to document the discussion. In doing so rather than approaching in a collaborative way, such as I had, he advised me to document my own ideas before capturing others. He told me that I influenced the discussion too indirectly because I asked questions of the others rather than telling them what we should do. His exact words were *"You have the pen; you have the power."*

While I could see the validity of this approach and scenarios where it would be advantageous to me to lead from the front in that manner, I paused to consider the specific situation that was observed. I shared my reflections with the senior leader and asked from his perspective did I still get to the outcome I desired. He agreed that ultimately, I did. So, I was a bit perplexed on why I had to shift my tactics in this situation to a more assertive, lead from the front approach when I accomplished my goal in a more inclusive, collaborative way.

This made me think, perhaps to be successful as a leader at the highest levels of an organization you need to be direct, assertive, and tell people what you think and what to do. I realized that if that was true then I did not aspire to advance my career to an executive level. If I were to adopt that type of leadership style in all, or even most, situations it would not be authentic and was in fact in direct conflict what not only worked for me but what I valued as key leadership qualities. However, rather than stall my career, I decided to apply this feedback when the situation called for it and be prepared to step up to lead using the power of the pen. Luckily, I was at a point in my professional growth that I could deeply consider feedback and find a way to use what is helpful and shed what was not.

I do not know whether I would have received comparable feedback from a female executive leader, or a younger executive leader, but I have experienced similar advice from other, more senior male leaders. Each time I heard it, I felt that if I were to fully implement the feedback, I would have lost the traits that make me an effective, empathetic leader whose purpose is to bring out the best in each of my team members. When feedback is delivered in a way that suggests without following the directions given you will not be successful, it becomes challenging to discard this "gift" you've been given. Especially for women who are still trying to gain equal footing and opportunity to accelerate their careers.

Diversity Lost?

When we give feedback to someone, we are teaching them to be more like us. We should really be trying to teach them to be more like them, the very best version of themselves that they can be. Others can benefit from our experiences and knowledge, there's no doubt. But how do we be sure they are not sacrificing who they are to follow our advice?

When we give feedback, our intention is usually to provide information to someone to change their behavior. The behavior may be something that's holding them back from being successful or damaging their reputation or relationships with others. I just caution in doing this, when we provide them with what to do instead, we are not only limiting their ability to come up with the solution that best works for them, but also may be denying a bit of what makes them unique and diverse.

Building a practice that draws their abilities and strengths out of them and helps them find the way that works for them to accomplish their goal is key. What works for you may not work for them. And we run the risk of losing that which makes them great by trying to mold them in our own form.

Conditioning our Feedback Response

These examples have one thing in common. They condition us on what to expect from feedback and therefore how to respond in the future. Over time, we begin to build up ways to protect ourselves from failure to avoid hearing feedback about our mistakes. These mechanisms become deeply ingrained forming obstacles blocking us from being truly open to hearing feedback. And even in the best circumstances, feedback can be uncomfortable and awkward.

This ties back to the fundamental feedback flaw #1, threat triggering. As you recall, our brains are wired for our survival and we learn how best to do this based upon our experiences, relying heavily on our amygdala to react appropriately to threats, both perceived and real.

To improve how we receive feedback we must overcome these protective mechanisms and learn to rewire the way we think about feedback. This can be done, no doubt, but requires the right motivation, maturity, and mindset to do so. Picture that each bad experience with feedback is a brick, and imagine how those bricks stack together over time erecting walls to prevent feedback from getting in. So, work must be done to chisel away at those bricks to allow us to embrace feedback for what it can be rather than how we may have experienced it in the past.

CHAPTER SEVEN

Expert Advice on How to Improve Feedback Experience

Applying what is known about neuroscience and the inherent feedback flaws, how can we improve the feedback experience? With so much research into this topic, there must be an answer, right? Maybe.

In this chapter, I will share some of these suggestions and ideas on how to get better at giving and receiving feedback. Each of these suggestions have merit along with shortcomings that we'll explore.

The Secret Sauce?

Any internet search on how to improve feedback will return an abundance of results. You will likely find suggestions such as encouraging everyone to ask for feedback rather than just wait to receive it, making sure there is psychological safety and a feedback culture, focusing feedback only on someone's strengths and not their weaknesses, and applying a mix of questions and advice. Many of these concepts leverage what we know about neuroscience and psychology to lessen the sting of feedback.

Approach #1

Let's take the first concept, asking for feedback. This approach gives the feedback receiver autonomy by being the one directing who and which feedback they receive. To understand this further we will look at West and Thorson's negotiation study.

In this study, participants engaged in mock negotiations and each side was tasked with giving feedback to each other following the negotiations. When the negotiations were completed, each side gave feedback on their opponent's performance; participants were randomly assigned to either request feedback or receive it without asking. They were equipped with heart rate monitors to track their pulse response.

Subjects in this study felt equally anxious receiving and giving feedback. In their study, West and Thorson discovered that participant's heart rates jumped as much as 50 percent, enough to indicate moderate or even extreme duress, particularly in the unprompted feedback situations. Spikes like this have been seen in stress provoking situations such as public speaking. Additionally, participants reported feelings of anxiety and uncertainty. They noticed that for those giving the feedback unsolicited, while rated as being friendlier than those who were asked to give it, their heart activity jumped around erratically, indicating discomfort and anxiety.[1]

The study asserts that when people request feedback there is a higher level of autonomy and certainty because they are in control. This proposes that feedback givers are also in a better place because they have more clarity around what type of feedback is needed. This is connected to the SCARF® model created by David Rock, founder and CEO of the NeuroLeadership Institute.

The SCARF® model includes five domains that impact how people feel and behave in social settings and as a part of a team or group: status, certainty, autonomy, relatedness, and fairness. The premise is that these aspects each have the potential to make us feel rewarded or threatened in that social situation.

- Status is the inclination we need to stand out from others, it's that feeling of importance.
- Certainty is the feeling of knowing what's going on and provide clarity to reduce ambiguity.
- Autonomy represents a sense of having some control over what we do.
- Relatedness is about feeling like we belong and are a part of something bigger than ourselves.
- Fairness is the desire for equality and equity in social situations.

So, in the approach outlined above, there are a few elements introduced that would create more psychological safety within the feedback experience, specifically autonomy, through being in control by asking for the feedback we want, and certainty, getting input to expand clarity.[23]

Though anchored to some solid concepts, there are a few limitations to this approach. Giving people control over requesting feedback is very empowering, but if people don't really want the feedback, they may either not ask or be very specific in what that they are looking to hear, and what they are not. Also, they may only limit input to people they know will be kind or provide primarily positive feedback which may not serve in providing insight into blind spots. Overall, encouraging people to actively seek feedback is a great idea, however restricting providing outside perspective only to when people ask for it runs the risk of being very limited in scope or perspective.

Approach #2

It's clear that psychological safety is an essential factor in the feedback equation. The safer someone feels to be themselves and as a result is able to trust in both the other person and the feedback process itself, the better the overall experience will be. This is very logical, and also may be impractical at times. Think about how many times we may need to address a situation or behavior with someone without having the benefit of the time and investment needed to create a truly psychologically safe environment.

    A blog from DDI, a global leadership consulting firm about why feedback fails in the workplace mentions the fight, flight, or freeze response, sharing that "everyone is afraid to make the wrong move, so leaders have simply stopped giving constructive feedback and performance issues go unaddressed" in an effort to not alienate talent.[24] The blog further states that by creating an environment of psychological safety feedback won't be perceived as a threat to an employee's sense of belonging. We explored the requirement for psychological safety in flaw #6. Creating an environment where people feel safe to fail and take risks, and that focuses on growth rather than criticism, is a clear way to minimize or avoid the threat response. In reality, it's not always possible to build that trusting relationship before needing to share an observation, or even when it is there, there is often still an element of discomfort and triggering of the amygdala.

If we can't always count on having already established trust and psychological safety, are we destined for discouraging and grim feedback experiences? Shortly, you will learn how to take what you've learned and shift your approach to achieve more effective and encouraging feedback experiences even in the absence of psychological safety.

Approach #3

To reduce the amount of threat triggering from feedback, another approach suggests building on what someone did well rather than focusing on what they didn't. The concept is that by doing more of what we do well we'll be more successful. Focusing on developing in areas of strength and finding ways to use those strengths to achieve our goals is a powerful tool.

This approach imagines "feedback that is more brain-friendly" by shifting the focus to what the person did well and should do more of. This puts the emphasis on what went right instead of what didn't. We know that our brains have more space dedicated to dealing with threats (like negative feedback) and we become intent on proving instead of improving ourselves.[25]

Gallup is a proponent of strength-based development, and their research indicates organizations that do this see 12.5% greater productivity and 8.9% greater profitability at

Expert Advice on How to Improve Feedback Experience

the team level as well as individuals being 6 times as likely to be engaged at work and 7.8% more productive in their role.[26]

In an article, Gallup shares that when employees receiving meaningful feedback in the past week, they are four times as likely to be engaged than other employees. But what does "meaningful" mean? According to Gallup, it's about giving feedback more frequently and keeping it brief, branding this as "Fast Feedback" and recommending also that it is more future oriented focusing on "how do we get even better." However, it still addresses an element of the past as seen in this example.[27]

"How do you think the presentation went? I noticed that the client had a few questions that seemed to indicate that they were not following along. What can we do next time to overcome that?"

This is likely more effective than other models we explored earlier but is still missing some key elements. The key to effective feedback from Gallup's perspective is for managers to "individualize feedback to employees' natural talents and performance needs." The strength-based development methodology has a lot to offer to improve the feedback experience, but there is opportunity to take this even further.

There is merit to this when it comes to development and achieving performance outcomes by leveraging your strengths and innate talents. In application from a feedback perspective, by strictly focusing on strengths, however, it would be easy to overlook or miss opportunities to shift behaviors that are causing negative impact to ourselves or others.

Approach #4

Several techniques have evolved to using an approach leveraging inquiry rather than being based solely on observation alone. Methods that embed questions into the feedback process can be effective in addressing some of the flaws acknowledged earlier. Let's look at some examples.

According to a 2019 Forbes Article, "Why Giving Feedback At Work Doesn't Improve Performance, And What You Can Do About It," there is a better way to improve performance than giving constructive feedback or offering the "feedback sandwich" we reviewed earlier. The suggestion is to simply shift from saying "Don't do that again" to "How might you do this better next time?" This is another powerful shift we can introduce to get us closer to a more effective conversation.[28] The examples within this article are an excellent reference point to thinking about how to better engage the feedback receiver in the dialogue and shut down the threat response by applying a more coach-like or question-based approach. This is heading in the right direction because it not only activates a more logical discussion over an emotional one but also begins to inspire some self-reflection, which I would argue should be the outcome of feedback, but more on that later. Per the article, some useful examples of how to put this in practice are as follows:

Expert Advice on How to Improve Feedback Experience

Instead of this...	*Say this...*
"You need to improve your communications."	"Based on what you know about working with Roger, how might you frame this differently to help him be more receptive?"
"Your strategy clearly didn't work."	"I'd like to hit this goal next time around. How do you think we can get there?"
"I don't understand why you can't meet deadlines."	"It's critical you meet this upcoming deadline because if you don't, the entire project will be disrupted. What do you need to do to make this happens?"

Similarly, there are some salient points in the *Harvard Business Review* article, "The Feedback Fallacy" that begins to highlight the flaws with a traditional feedback approach.[8] Beyond exposing some limiting beliefs feedback is rooted in, the article shares sample language that can be used to help colleagues excel (see below). You'll see integration of more questions, as in the prior example which helps address some of the threat response that feedback triggers, and we'll discuss that in a bit more detail later. You will also see a bit of flipping messages from advising someone on what to do to sharing what you would do or what has worked for you, not them. This is good to have in the ready for when someone is stuck and can't see a path forward, but when we give them our version of the answers, we are depriving them of the benefit gained by learning how to find them by turning to what is within instead of outside of themselves.

Instead of	Try
Can I give you some feedback?	Here's my reaction.
Good job!	Here are three things that really worked for me. What was going through your mind when you did them?
Here's what you should do.	Here's what I would do.
Here's where you need to improve.	Here's what worked best for me, and here's why.
That didn't really work.	When you did x, I felt y, or I didn't get that.
You need to improve your communication skills.	Here's exactly where you started to lose me.
You need to be more responsive.	When I don't hear from you, I worry that we're not on the same page.
You lack strategic thinking.	I'm struggling to understand your plan.
You should do x [in response to a request for advice].	What do you feel you're struggling with, and what have you done in the past that's worked in a similar situation?

Expert Advice on How to Improve Feedback Experience

Building on Expert Advice

There are viable options offered in the approaches and advice above. When we start to tap into brain science and psychology, we can learn to create a more engaging feedback experience. Let's continue to explore that with the concept of coaching which was touched on a bit in some of the approaches above.

CHAPTER EIGHT

How a Coaching Approach is a Step in the Right Direction

In this chapter we'll explore coaching and define what it is and what it isn't. We'll look at coaching compared to feedback as we find a better way forward to engage with others in perspective sharing.

What Is Coaching?

When you hear the word "coach" what do you think of? Likely when you think of a coach it's in the context of a sports coach or perhaps a teacher, someone who has shared their knowledge with you to help you learn and improve. We tend to group people who train, instruct, or advise into our definition of coach. When asked to define a coach, a common response is someone who guides players and directs team strategy. Most of us have experienced a coach in this way through sports or education.

There is another definition of coaching I would like to introduce. The International Coaching Federation, the leading global organization for coaches and coaching, defines

How a Coaching Approach is a Step in the Right Direction

coaching as "partnering with clients in a thought-provoking and creative process that inspires them to maximize their personal and professional potential. The process of coaching often unlocks previously untapped sources of imagination, productivity and leadership."[29]

What do you notice about the nuance between these definitions? The first one is about *pushing* knowledge and experience to the coachee while the second one is about *pulling* knowledge and experience from the coachee. The big difference here is an approach that relies on telling someone what to do versus asking someone questions to help them discover what to do.

This may get a bit confusing because our experience with coaches more likely corresponds to the first definition, however that traditional coaching definition aligns better with the concept of a mentor. And perhaps you've had mentors. When you think about a coach and mentor do you use those words interchangeably? Most people do. However, a different way to think about it is that what we've experienced from a coaching perspective is actually mentoring. I came across a very simple way to look at mentoring and coaching from the Air Force. I used their concepts to put together this comparison:

Mentor

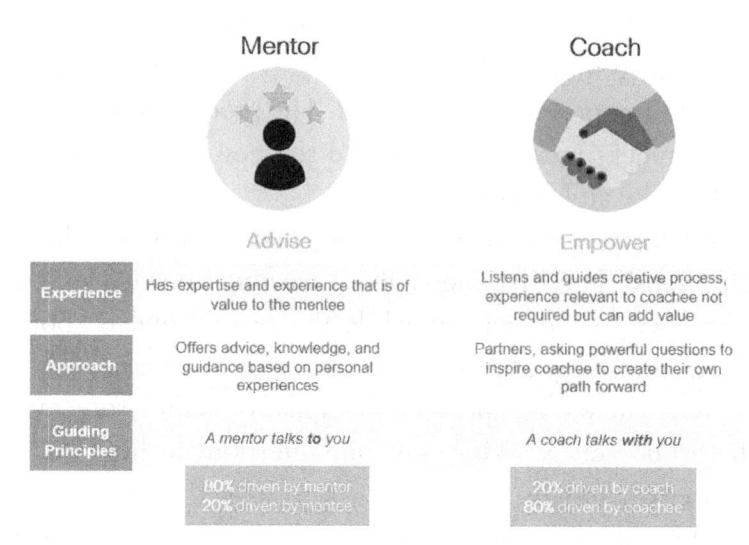

Advise

Experience	Has expertise and experience that is of value to the mentee
Approach	Offers advice, knowledge, and guidance based on personal experiences
Guiding Principles	A mentor talks **to** you
	80% driven by mentor / 20% driven by mentee

Coach

Empower

Experience	Listens and guides creative process, experience relevant to coachee not required but can add value
Approach	Partners, asking powerful questions to inspire coachee to create their own path forward
Guiding Principles	A coach talks **with** you
	20% driven by coach / 80% driven by coachee

***Mentor vs Coach:** I love this simple comparison to differentiate mentoring and coaching as we think of them interchangeably, when they are distinct[30]*

This way of thinking about coaching stems from different description of a coach, which is a large carriage used for transportation purposes. If you are struggling to see the connection, think of it as simply a way to get someone *from where they are* now to *where they want to be.*

***Coach:** image of wheeled carriage used to transport people[31]*

So, for the purpose of this book, when I talk about coaching, I mean coaching as a tool to listen and ask productive questions to guide the creative process for the coachee.

Why Coaching?

Adopting a more coach-like approach opens up our brains to those "aha moments" because it engages our brain's logic and reasoning center, the prefrontal cortex. This large area of the brain is associated with performing various complex tasks. The prefrontal cortex is "a part of the frontal lobe in our brain responsible for an array of vital functions, including executive functioning, memory, attention, and emotion regulation."[32]

Connecting to the neuroscience we've already begun exploring let's tie it all together now. We've discussed the amygdala, an area of the brain that is "constantly alert to the needs of basic survival" and the role it plays in how we respond to feedback.[33] When threat is detected, our amygdala sounds the alarm, triggering the release of stress hormones, like cortisol and adrenaline, in response. These hormones serve to prepare us to address the threat. Adrenaline functions in several ways, causing our pupils to dilate to enhance our vison and contracting our blood vessels to redirect blood to our muscles in preparation for fight or flight.[34] The frontal lobe is the part of our brains that has most recently evolved and is the last to fully develop into early adulthood. Its role in executive functioning helps to regulate our emotional responses and think clearly. When we engage our prefrontal cortex, we can more effectively assess the threat our amygdala has identified and make a rational decision on how to best respond, rather than a response distorted by our emotions only.

When our amygdala is activated it "immediately shuts down the neural pathway to our prefrontal cortex" and therefore "complex decision making disappears, as does our access to multiple perspectives."[35] This means that our ability to use our reasoning center (the prefrontal cortex) to evaluate the emotions triggered by the amygdala is not available to us in this moment. The response by our amygdala is involuntary while the frontal lobes process the threat and may override the amygdala so you can approach the situation more rationally than automatically. The amygdala and prefrontal cortex "work together concerning the stress response system; the amygdala signals the presence of stress or threat and the prefrontal cortex assists the amygdala in assessing the situation in a less threatening perspective."[36]

If we think about the amygdala as an alarm system dialed to detect threats to our safety we can think of the prefrontal cortex as a way to tune that alarm and determine a logical response, even if the response is not to respond at all. We learned that receiving feedback is often perceived as a threat by the amygdala, so how do we leverage that knowledge and what we now know about the prefrontal cortex to better regulate our emotional response to that uncomfortable situation? This is where coaching can be effective.

Coaching leverages effective listening techniques paired with powerful questions to generate reflection and new thinking in the coachee. Research has shown that when asked a question the human brain is wired to search for an answer. For example, if I ask how old you are, you are likely to think of your current age. This seems like a basic example but what it tells us is how our brains respond when we are asked a question. You didn't direct your brain to think about your age, it just did. When we are thinking about the answer to a question our brains cannot consider anything else at the same time.[37]

Additionally, the coaching process of asking questions engages the logical center, the prefrontal cortex, allowing a more calm, logical approach to an obstacle or problem we're working through. So, our brains are wired to find an answer to the question from a coach and we are also activating our prefrontal cortex to work toward calming down any emotions that may be currently clouding our vision to help create more clarity in our thinking.

What is amazing about this is that until a few decades ago it was believed that our brain's growth was limited, as represented by the saying "you can't teach an old dog a new trick." Turns out, you can! Our view of this has evolved and we know now that our brains are constantly changing throughout our lives in response to internal and external stimuli. In this process, called neuroplasticity, our brains are creating new neural pathways, new connections between neurons, in response to our experiences, emotions, behaviors and thoughts.

Coaches support their coachees in what neuroscientist Jeffrey Schwartz calls self-directed neuroplasticity (SDN). SDN suggests that we can change the physical structure and functions of our brains with intentional thought and focus.[38] Coaching aids in SND, one's own ability to "rewire" our brain, through guiding the redirection of thoughts and construction of new thought patterns that better serve the coachee.

The benefit to coaching is it uses various techniques like asking questions and reframing and challenging thoughts and memories of the coachee to help drive breakthroughs. By asking questions and activating the brain's desire to seek an answer, coaching engages the prefrontal cortex and therefore focuses on more stimulating thinking from a more logical rather than emotional foundation. The amygdala quiets down as perceived threats are deemed benign, and we can use the power within our logic brain to create a path forward for ourselves. Ultimately coaching is a tool that can calm our threat response whereas feedback is likely to trigger it.

Coaching in Principle

There are a few principles that serve as a foundation for coaching.

Principle #1: The agenda is set by the coachee. This is a significant distinction from feedback, where typically the agenda is determined by the feedback giver. You'll recall that the purpose of feedback is for the feedback giver to provide information and insight to the feedback receiver. As a result, in most cases the agenda for the feedback discussion is driven by the giver. In the situations where the feedback receiver proactively requests specific feedback, they may drive the agenda more. However, in coaching, the topic of discussion is decided by the coachee and the coach's role is to ensure that the coach clearly defines what they want to get from the discussion.

Setting the agenda requires tapping into what the coachee needs and wants. The coach is to set aside their own thoughts

How a Coaching Approach is a Step in the Right Direction

and focus on creating a structured discussion in which the agenda is up to the coachee. The role of the coach is to help keep the conversation on track and productive to meet the agenda and goals of the coachee.

Principle #2: Follow the 80/20 rule where the coach listens 80% and speaks 20%. The coach applies active listening and utilizes only a small portion of the airtime to ask questions, reflect back what they heard, and offer their own observations. As outlined above, the purpose is to create the space for which the coachee can talk through their goals and challenges.

This requires really being present and engaging effective listening techniques. This can be challenging because our minds are primed to solve problems and as we hear from the coachee it is natural to begin formulating questions or advice for them rather than just tuning in and really listening. Also, we have a tendency to want to share what we know and our opinions, so this principle requires us to refrain from dominating the discussion or sharing our thoughts without being asked to. Coaches may offer observations or advice, but it should be limited and up to the coach to decide what is of value to them.

Principle #3: Use mostly open-ended, non-leading questions to spark thought and insight within the coachee. An open-ended question is one which cannot be answered with yes or no. Leveraging question starters like what, when, how, and where are key to this approach. Another suggestion is to avoid beginning a question with "why" as that can be perceived as a threat and trigger a defensive response.

One common challenge with this principle is that the "why" question is one that tends to pop into our head and as a coach we seek to reframe that using another word even if at times starting with "why" may be acceptable. Additionally, a common misstep of coaches is to disguise advice in the form of a question. That could like something like this, rather than asking "what have you tried already to address your concerns" or "how might you align with that stakeholder," we say "have you scheduled a meeting with John to address your concerns" or "have you tried talking to the stakeholder and asking them what they need from you." These close-ended questions don't follow the principle and are just recommendations in the form of a question attempting to lead the coachee toward a particular action or solution.

Principle #4: Coaches should be non-judgmental. To create an open, collaborative space between the coach and coachee, a coach needs to suspend judgment. A great deal of practice and energy is required to master this principle as a human with innate biases and a brain wired for judgment. We naturally make judgment-based decisions about the thoughts, emotions, and actions of other people. Applying this principle often takes constant monitoring and silencing of our inner judges.

Sound familiar? This is very similar to feedback principle #7 to be objective when you give feedback. We already explored the challenge with that in reality, which applies with coaching to an extent as well.

This can show up either as deeming something as worthy or right because it aligns with our own value systems and beliefs. Alternately, if a coachee is expressing an opinion or action that is not aligned with our actions or beliefs our inner judge will emerge to express disagreement or even disgust. Over time an effective coach can learn how to dampen their judgment or may end up stepping away from a relationship if they feel they cannot do so.

Principle #5: Coaching is goal-bound and action-oriented. All coaching should be anchored to a goal set by the coachee. This is tied to the principle of the coachee deciding the agenda but takes it even further. The role of the coach is to urge the coachee to clearly articulate their goal in the terms of what they want, not what they don't want. A simple example of this is if a coachee says, "I don't want to be overweight anymore," the coach would ask them what they do want, "I want to be healthy and in good shape." The coach would then prompt for more clarity around the goal, possibly using the SMART concept developed by George Doran, Arthur Miller and James Cunningham in 1981. This is acronym represents defining a goal in a way that is specific, measurable, attainable, realistic, and timely (with a specific timeline identified). This would help define what "healthy" means and what does "good shape" look like for the coachee.

The coach should ensure that adequate time is dedicated to defining the goal so that the coachee can clearly articulate it, since you cannot meet a goal you don't know how to measure. The goal should be continually reevaluated and progress toward the goal should be assessed during the coaching process. The coach will then have the coachee decide on specific actions that they feel will help them move toward their goal. Both goal and related actions will be defined and owned by the coachee with the coach acting as a sounding board to test how challenging but realistic and achievable they are. The coach will also act as an accountability partner as needed to check-in with.

Principle #6: Everything the coachee needs to be successful can be found within them. This principle advocates that the coachee is fully capable of solving their own problems and achieving their goals, they are not a problem to be solved by the coach.

The role of the coach is to guide the process of self-reflecting and to spark new ideas and thoughts simply through asking those questions and mirroring what they are hearing. The coach can help challenge any limiting beliefs or actions that are not moving the coachee toward their goal.

Coaching Models

Just like with feedback, there are several models to support a coaching conversation. The purpose of these models is to help structure and frame the discussion in alignment with the above coaching principles. I will share a few to provide context around how a coaching conversation may be accomplished using one of these structured approaches.

One of the most broadly used model is **GROW**. First developed by John Whitmore in the 1980s, it represents:

- **Goal**: define the coachee's goal.
- **Reality**: discuss of the current state the coachee is in.
- **Options**: explore of possible options that could help achieve the defined goal.

- **Will**: select the specific actions the coachee will take to move forward and confirm their commitment to progress their action plan. Alternatively, I have seen the "W" denoted as "wrap-up" or "way forward" as well.

This model is often used in organizational coaching models because it is easy to remember and apply. The coachee is asked to define their goal in terms of the SMART acronym. The coach then asks questions for the coachee to describe the current state; what is happening, for how long, what have they tried already. The model then moves them into brainstorming possible options that the coachee could take to achieve their goal. The last step is to identify which of those options the coachee wants to commit to and for them to describe the specific actions they will take and by when they will take them.

The **CLEAR** model was developed by Peter Hawkins in the early 1980s and is a feasible alternative to the GROW model. The model is as follows:[41]

- **Contract**: identify the desired outcomes and discuss the coaching process.
- **Listen**: the coach listens and engages only to guide the conversation toward the agreed upon goal.
- **Explore**: examine the effect of the situation on the coachee.
- **Action**: align on actions and changes the coachee will commit to.
- **Review**: continue discussions to follow up and check on progress or challenges the coachee is encountering.

Another coaching model is **OSCAR**, which was initially described by Gilbert and Whittleworth in 2002. This model concentrates on the solution and not the problem.[41]

- **Outcome**: define the desired outcome and coachee's goals.
- **Situation**: create awareness of the coachee's abilities, strengths, and feelings.
- **Choices**: consider what options are available to reach the desired outcome.
- **Actions**: select which improvements are needed and how to achieve them.
- **Reviews**: hold regular progress reviews to ensure the client is on track.

Despite minor differences in these three models, overall, they are fairly similar. These similarities are obvious, and ultimately all encouraging clear articulation of the goal, examination of the current state and commitment to actions to move them toward their goal. Just as with feedback, there are many coaching models. The purpose of the model is to bring structure and incorporate the principles to support effective coaching conversations.

Coaching and Feedback

We've explored what coaching is, why coaching is a valuable method to support moving someone from where they are to where they want to be, and considered different approaches to conduct a coaching conversation.

Both coaching and feedback have a place. They each serve a specific purpose. Put simply, feedback is about

How a Coaching Approach is a Step in the Right Direction

providing input while coaching is about getting output. The intent of feedback is to provide your opinion and ideas to someone else to consider, apply, and adjust their behavior accordingly. On the other hand, coaching strives to seek the answers and thoughts of the other person with the belief that they are fully capable of finding their own path forward rather than you providing them with your way forward. Feedback is about you; coaching is about them. Feedback tends to be about pushing your thoughts to someone to minimize the negative impact they are having on you, while coaching is about listening to the other person and drawing insights from them.

We know that experiencing feedback can trigger our amygdala and therefore results in biological and chemical reactions preparing us for a fight, flight, or freeze response. Coaching helps to reduce that biological response by engaging our prefrontal cortex and tapping into our powerful logic center to better regulate the emotional response.

The challenge is we see these as separate tools and abilities, while the better we tie these together the more effective our conversations will be. We absolutely will need to share our opinions and information with other people so that we can help expand their perspective and reduce their blind spots. We should also have times where we can tap into their own brilliance and ability to solve problems and find ways forward. Both feedback and coaching are necessary, so the question remains, how do we leverage the best of these and have more effective, powerful discussions to aid in the growth and discovery of each other?

In my experience, most people convolute feedback and coaching. They say they are coaching other people, while in reality, they are actually providing feedback and mentorship as we outlined before. Even those who understand what coaching means may struggle to deliver it. We'll approach a situation and define it either as a "feedback" discussion or a "coaching" discussion. While the best approach is to merge the methods to engage in more compelling conversations where the outcome is deeper insight and self-awareness through reflection and perspective sharing.

CHAPTER NINE

Creating Dynamic Dialogues

We're finally here! In this chapter you will learn how to move from *confrontation* to *conversation*. We'll talk about how to flip the model we've explored in feedback to drive more self-reflection, effectively "teaching someone to fish." We'll look at how to take a more human-centered approach using empathetic inquiry to learn how talk to each other and share perspectives. Our goal is to create a culture of self-reflection not feedback, feedback is just one of the ways to broaden our self-awareness.

Flip the Focus

The approaches we've learned to take to give feedback and develop others is one where we depend heavily on feedback, lesser on coaching, and even less on prompting introspection. Which looks something like this:

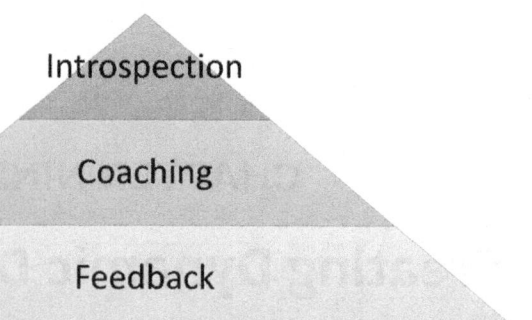

Pyramid diagram with three layers from top to bottom: Introspection, Coaching, Feedback.

Image courtesy of author

However, if we can flip that, leveraging more inquiry to gain deeper understanding of someone's perspectives, thoughts, beliefs, and values, we can create a better way to approach understanding where they are and helping them to move forward. Consider how to inspire more self-reflection and open their awareness though asking questions. Flipping the model puts the focus on introspection and highlights coaching and feedback as paths toward that more enlightened, self-aware state. Feedback becomes supplementary rather than primary.

Inverted pyramid diagram with three layers from top to bottom: Introspection, Coaching, Feedback.

Image courtesy of author

Empathetic Inquiry

What if instead of providing our opinion and thoughts we approached the situation with an open mind and open heart? What if we expressed an interest in what the other person had to say and made sure they felt heard and understood? What do you think the difference could be in the outcome of the discussion and the experience to get there? I propose we leverage an empathetic inquiry approach to position ourselves to better understand and listen to the other person's perspective.

Empathy is becoming a more critical skill as we seek out ways to build deeper, more meaningful, connections with others. Empathy is having an awareness of the thoughts and feelings that others are experiencing, to the point that you may even be able to sense and share in them. Through empathy we can appreciate the experiences and emotions of others vicariously, even if we have never experienced them ourselves. Empathy often gets confused with sympathy. Think of it this way, sympathy is feeling sorry *for* you; empathy is feeling sorry *with* you.

Inquiry can be defined as requesting information. Inquiry is categorized by asking questions to examine, investigate, or understand.

Putting these together results in a process to gain deeper understanding of another person through asking questions. In this we want to know what the person is thinking and feeling and figure out how those thoughts and emotions play a role in their actions and behaviors.

This requires intentionality and thought. We can start by setting aside our assumptions and judgments. Recall, as humans, we are quick to make value judgments and assume we know better or would behave differently. While this may be true, rather than judging the person's actions, thoughts, or beliefs as "good" or "bad," consider they just are. They are theirs to own and for us to acknowledge and perhaps challenge only if they limit them from moving forward to their goal. Perhaps we do know better and would not have acted or made the same decision that they did, but we all work to make decisions from the place we are currently and what we've learned up until now. Rather than assume what they did was wrong or bad, assume that we don't know all the answers and should seek to uncover them together.

Be curious. Curiosity helps us set aside our judgments and assumptions. When we crave to learn and understand more, we can set aside that "know-best bias" that was highlighted earlier. Maybe, just maybe, we don't know it all. Consider what you could ask to open that door to better understanding.

As you listen, seek to understand, and not just respond. This is where the active listening comes to play as you immerse yourself in learning more about the person to expand your own understanding and not to contradict what they are saying. Your questions should help uncover insights for both of you to learn and move forward.

Empathetic inquiry requires us to metaphorically put ourselves in someone else's shoes. To think about the situation not from where we sit and our lived experiences, expertise, and knowledge, but from theirs. When we can connect on this level, we are better positioned to help them navigate a path forward, blending the best of coaching and feedback to ask powerful questions, acknowledge what we've heard, challenge limiting beliefs, thoughts, or actions, and share our perspective as well.

Let's Talk!

Throughout this book I've highlighted what makes giving and receiving feedback so hard. And how coaching, which is intended to minimize the emotional response, can be difficult to execute well. I mentioned taking a blended approach and stop thinking about having a "feedback" discussion or "coaching" conversation, and just talking to people. Leaning into the empathetic inquiry approach to drive a more human-centered exchange. So, how do we do that?

We can apply the principles of **TALK**, to create this open sharing of perspectives and ideas. Because, really, while there is right and wrong, there are often also infinite shades of gray between. There is also the element of relativity, what may have worked for you, may not for someone else. What may be a good action in one situation may not be in another. Using **TALK and empathetic inquiry we can find the best way forward for the person based on who and where they are now.**

TALK stands for **Think, Ask, Listen,** and **Know.** TALK is about inspiring **dynamic dialogues** in which both people share their perspectives and are appreciated for what they bring to the discussion. This approach blends feedback and coaching to reduce the threat response and inspire self-reflection by asking questions balanced with providing your own insights and advice. The goal is to engage the other person in the conversation and to expand their perspective as well as your own.

TALK is not a rigid model like the others we've explored. It is not about applying this model and following it to deliver feedback or even coaching. Recall how we talked about those models being helpful to structure our thinking but in reality, they each fall short in some aspect? In a dynamic dialogue these are prompts for you to consider as a guide to navigating a better way to deliver feedback. I consider this just sharing your perspective, which should be based on your own observable facts. But you know the saying there are three sides to every story? Yours, mine, and the truth. As much as we try to be truthful in our observations, we are also human and there may be gaps or flaws in our recollection. And we certainly can't claim to fully understand another's thoughts or intentions. In a dynamic dialogue we have the chance to explore this and adjust the conversation based upon how the discussion unfolds. Let's dig into the principles of TALK.

Think: prepare for your conversation thinking about what outcome you want from it and the best way to approach achieving that outcome. Think about how you can leverage an empathetic inquiry approach and what you need to say and want to better understand the other person. Consider how to make it a dialogue in which you each have perspectives to share. What questions will you ask? How will you share your own perspective and observations? Think is all about considering how to best approach the situation in which you need to provide someone with feedback.

To help you with this here are a few tips:

Test your judgments and assumptions. As you prepare ask yourself what you know to be true, what assumptions are you making, and other questions to help you set aside your biases and assumptions. For example, in the case we explored earlier with a team member who was on their phone during a team meeting you probably have some assumptions going in. You may think that he was disrespectful or bored by the conversation. You may assume that his intentions were not good or that he simply didn't care about the impact his behavior may have had on the team. You may assume that everyone was put off by his actions. Really, all you know is that in a team meeting he checked his phone a number of times and seemed to be texting or being involved with the phone. You do not know that he didn't listen to the meeting, you do not know whether there was a reason for him to be on the phone. This is where sticking to the facts is important and we should follow the principles of feedback in terms of identifying what we saw, heard, or even felt without assigning blame or judgment.

Tune into your own emotions. Remember giving feedback or initiating a difficult conversation is just as challenging for the person who is the giver as it is for the receiver. You will likely have some stress responses if you are called to share your observation with someone else, particularly so if you are discussing a problematic situation or anticipating a challenging response from the person. Take a moment to tap into how you are feeling, acknowledge it, and take some deep breaths. It's ok to be nervous, but the more you approach as a conversation the easier it becomes. It's also perfectly fine to pause or reschedule a discussion if you or the other person isn't in the right emotional state to be productive.

Trust that the other person has experiences and knowledge. They may already be aware of the situation and what they could have done differently. If they are not, you will have an opportunity to provide insight to help them see other perspectives and expand their awareness. Also, trust that most likely their intentions were not bad or malicious. Of course, this isn't always the case as you will have plenty of conflicts in your life with people who are trying to hurt your feelings and even if that's the case you can navigate that with focusing on a conversation and exchange of viewpoints.

Tact is key to success. Being tactful isn't always easy, so this is a good thing to think about as you prepare for the conversation. Being tactful means that you are able to share the truth and facts in a way that is sensitive to how others may feel or react. If you share the observable facts without judgment or assumption this becomes much easier.

Consider an example you've likely come across; someone has something in their teeth. This can be embarrassing. So much that people don't always let others know that there is something in their teeth, or maybe indirectly address through checking their own teeth hoping the other person gets a hint. What if instead, we just said, "John, I thought you'd want to know there is something in your teeth." John may still be slightly embarrassed, because that's human nature, but we have not implied judgment in our factual observation.

Together you can move forward. Many feedback discussions I've been a part of or have been shared with me by others have a feeling of "me" vs "them." In some ways this is part of that stress response as our brain prepares us to deal with the perceived threat. If we feel attacked, it is almost impossible for us to rationally see validity in what someone is saying. However, if we approach in a way that builds affiliation and asserts that we are there to work through this together, it can go a long way to opening up the dialogue.

To best prepare, think about your goal for the discussion, what is it that you want to accomplish. Do your best to set aside your assumptions and judgements, tap into your emotions and be aware of them so you can approach from a logical place, consider the person may already have some awareness, be thoughtful of their own feelings as you share just the facts, and contemplate how to be a partner to help forge a way forward together with the other person.

Ask: open the conversation with a question and share your intent. For example, I'd like to debrief on that meeting yesterday, when would be a good time? Remember, the approach offered for feedback to ask, "may I offer some feedback?" You could still apply a similar approach if the situation is one where you are ok if the person says no. In this case you would frame it like this, "I'd love to share my thoughts with you if you are open to it," or "May I share my observations with you?"

Also, ask them about what their thoughts and reflections are before you share yours. You could ask something like, "How do you think that meeting went?" or "What did you feel went well?" and "What didn't go so well?" This is applying the coaching mindset where your primary role is prompt self-reflection and to then to help fill in any gaps or alternative perspectives you have to add.

Agree to the agenda. Set your intentions and align on what you'd like to accomplish from the discussion. Remember, the purpose of these discussions should always be to spark self-reflection first and then offer your insights and experience to broaden their awareness. So, the agenda could be to reflect on the meeting and learn from what went well and identify some actions to improve next time. Or it could just be to talk about what didn't go so well and focus on what are some alternative actions to have a better meeting outcome next time. Your questions and thoughts should only help to advance that agenda.

Align on the goals. As you continue the discussion, any actions identified should be aligned to the goals and achieving the desired outcome. Whether that's improving the meeting outcome or better engaging in the discussion to listen and contribute, the overall goal is what comes next. What will we walk away from the conversation doing, thinking, or saying differently?

Acknowledge their perspectives. When we start by asking for the other person's thoughts and reflections it opens up the dialogue for us. They may already be aware of a behavior that wasn't acceptable or created an unintended impact on themselves or others. This allows us to reinforce and share our own similar perspective to help them address that behavior. By acknowledging their perspective, we are validating that they are human and it's ok for them to have an off day or make a mistake. Even if it is a mistake that has been discussed repeatedly, acknowledging how they are feeling about this can help bring about growth within the other person. You will also share your own perspective, and by acknowledging you heard and understood theirs, they are more likely to do the same for you.

Adapt to the conversation flow as needed. You may need to abandon your agenda if the conversation isn't addressing it in a productive way or you see another topic that is better served by the discussion. Be willing to let go of the feedback you wanted to share if you find it becomes irrelevant or incorrect based on having limited information. Again, you may find that through opening the dialogue for the other person to share their thoughts you may not need to go deeply into yours, so be ready to adapt.

Listen: now that you've thought of how to best engage in a conversation and open with questions to encourage the other person to share their own thoughts and reflections, it's time to listen. Sounds easy, right? Most of the time we listen to respond rather than listen to understand. Thoughts and responses will pop into your head as the other person is speaking. Set them aside and pay attention to what they are saying. Once you understand their perspective you can better frame your next question or position your response accordingly.

Learn what the other person thinks and what matters to them. Be curious and recognize that you don't know everything. You may have great instincts and insights, but humans are complex, and every discussion is an opportunity to learn. Taking this approach addresses the "know-best" bias we covered earlier. By staying curious and seeking to understand you can combat our natural affinity of being the expert.

Logical dialogue is the goal. By asking questions and be genuinely curious we can help deactivate the threat response and stimulate the brain's logic center. Also, by acknowledging the emotions that are there rather than saying things like "don't be upset," or "it's not a big deal" can help deflate those emotions given some time. Stay in touch with your own emotions as well, recognize that if the conversation is difficult or there is an emotional reaction from the other person it's likely your own emotions will be triggered in response. Take a pause as needed to acknowledge your emotions as well as the other person's. You can even learn to self-coach in this moment, asking yourself questions like how is this moving us toward our goal, or what can I do to make this discussion more productive.

Look for connections you can make to bridge your perspectives, especially if they are in conflict. One thing I have found helpful is saying something like, I understand where you're coming from and I see it differently, or I have a different opinion or thought. Or thank them for sharing their thoughts with you before you offer your own. Acknowledging their perspective and recognizing that you have an alternative view is a good start. You may find that the person is already self-aware and may actually be harder on themselves that you would be. We're often our own worst critic. Either way, seek out ways to connect your perspectives and look for how their perspective can expand your thinking not just yours to expand theirs.

Lift the other person. Giving feedback should be about helping the other person. And most of the time that is our intent. But sometimes we use it to tell someone to be more like us and what we deem appropriate or acceptable behavior instead of being a better version of themselves. The more you understand who they are and what their strengths are the better you can tailor any advice or insights you offer them. An example of this is a team member who thrives on getting information and details before they get started on a project. This helps them understand how best to move forward and create the impact they desire. However, there are times when the information they want simply isn't available when we need to begin. So rather than telling them, "You need to move faster, you don't need that information," I ask questions like, "What information do you need to get started?" and "What steps can you take right now?" Honoring how someone is wired and the strengths that make them successful is a great way to help them navigate when those strengths may be getting in the way of their success. Usually, it's our greatest strengths that become our biggest obstacles when we lean on them too heavily or don't balance them with other strengths. By appealing to their strengths, we can lift them up with the conversation rather than bringing them down which can be an outcome of a feedback discussion. Understanding that we all have different strengths that we leverage to achieve an outcome is a good way to tap into how the person can best solve the challenge ahead using their strengths. It also allows us to gain insight into the behavior we observed.

Know: the goal of any feedback or coaching discussions is knowledge. And ultimately the more that that knowledge can be sparked from within the other person, the better. Remember, we want to help people learn to fish rather than give them a fish. We have knowledge we want to share in the discussion. The other person also has knowledge that we can tap into. When both parties walk away from the discussion learning something, it has been a success.

Keep the dialogue productive. If at any time you, or the other person, feels like you are not making progress toward the agenda and goal that you've agreed to, step back. Despite using the tactics above to ask questions, acknowledge emotions and different perspectives, and honor the person's knowledge, you may still find that the conversation feels confrontational or heated. In this case, the best thing to do is pause. You can call out the elephant in the room rather than ignore it. I've used language like, "This conversation doesn't feel like we're making progress, should we pause and come back to it later?" or "We've come to a place that isn't very productive, let's take some time to reflect on our own and connect further at a later time." I have even been more blunt and said, "It seems as if we're both really frustrated right now, why don't we take some time apart to cool off."

Kindness is crucial. We talked about tact which is essentially a combination of truth and kindness. Usually, we tend to go toward one or the other. We deliver truth in a fact-based manner that is logical but could feel cold or unfeeling to the other person. Or we are kind and choose to skirt around the issue and end up being indirect and miss making our point. Which is why I like the concept of being tactful. That said, kindness is a great mindset to approach a conversation with. If you are not coming from a place of kindness or concern for the other person, it will be more about you than them. This can be challenging especially if someone's behavior is hurting you in some way. Or if you've already judged them to be "a jerk" or worse. But if you can set aside that judgment and think about how to be open to their perspective and assume positive intent instead you can get in a good frame of mind to have the dialogue.

Knit the story together. During your discussion, you may find yourselves all over the place. When you hear what the other person is saying and acknowledge it you can start to knit everything together. This is where you tie both perspectives together. When you can share back what you've heard or understood from the other person you can paint the full picture. This is where you bring in both perspectives and define the truth coming out of the discussion.

Kindle their passion. What are they excited about? What are their personal or professional goals? What really matters to them? Consider these as you continue your dialogue. Traditional feedback is about pushing your perspective onto someone else, and it rarely connects to what they need or want. When done well, we can make that connection. For example, if someone has a professional goal and our feedback is specific to helping them achieve that, it is usually more well received because we connect to what is important to them, vs. what is important to us. In these dynamic dialogues, when we talk to them about what's important to them and understand their goals, we can direct the conversation in a much more productive way to spark excitement within them as they are growing toward their goal.

Kudos! As you wrap the conversation be sure to thank them. A simple thank you goes a long way. Regardless of the type of relationship you have with the person, if they are your child, if they report directly to you, if you are in a place of authority, if you are expected to give them feedback – thank them. Do this in a way that is authentic to you and to the flow of the conversation. It doesn't have to be at the end of the discussion. Just acknowledge that they took the time to listen to your thoughts or share their own thinking with you. I have said things like, "I appreciate your time today" or "thank you for listening to my perspective."

Why Give Feedback When You Can Just Talk?

There will be times when you need to give quick, immediate feedback. For example, if there is some behavior that you need to redirect quickly to prevent a serious issue or harm, feedback will be needed. I consider this as a situation like my son is about to chase a ball into the street and there is a car coming. If there is real danger involved, by no means do you want to take the time to have a dialogue.

Besides those times, consider when you can realistically substitute feedback with a dynamic dialogue. Using empathetic inquiry to explore someone else's perspective rather than push your perspective upon them can minimize or eliminate our emotional response triggered by feedback. Using this method, you can address the fundamental flaws of feedback and still be direct and clear in sharing your point of view.

Earlier, we went through several examples of the impact feedback can have. It can create a long-lasting negative association for feedback discussions that may limit our ability to hear and appreciate the opinions of others in the future. Sometimes the feedback experience drives a hyper-focus on not making mistakes again, which is unrealistic. When we use an empathetic inquiry approach, we can counter many, and perhaps even all, of the flaws we outlined and reduce the negative, lasting impact on people.

Let's play this out using the example we established earlier: your team member John was in a team meeting and was on his phone during much of the conversation.

"Hi John, when you have a few minutes can we touch base on the team meeting yesterday?"

"Sure, let's talk now."

"Great. How did you think the meeting went?"

"It was ok. I really didn't have a lot to add."

"What makes you say that?"

"Well, the discussion was about a topic that I have little expertise in. I honestly tuned out a bit."

"The purpose of our team meetings is to learn about the team's work and share ideas with each other. I wonder if you would have been able to contribute more as the conversation progressed into other topics. From our prior discussions, I know you have some ideas to share."

"Maybe."

"I noticed that you seemed to be on your phone during parts of the conversation. How might that have distracted you from the topics discussed?"

"I did have a few other things going on, so I probably was distracted."

"What else was on your plate that was distracting you during the meeting?"

"My son hurt himself at school yesterday right before our meeting, so I was texting my wife during the meeting."

"No wonder you needed to be on the phone! How is he doing?"

"He's fine but he broke his arm, and my wife took him to the hospital. She was letting me know what was going on."

"John, thank you for sharing that with me. What do you need from me?"

"I may need to take some time off to get him to some of his doctor's appointments."

"Absolutely, take the time you need. I'm so glad your son is doing ok. You must have been so worried when you found out he was injured."

"Thank you. I felt bad about missing parts of the meeting. I should have excused myself to call my wife rather than being distracted trying to text her back and forth. I was just worried and didn't think I could just leave our meeting."

"Anytime you need to step away from work or out of a meeting to handle family emergencies, we will understand. Prioritize your family and yourself so that when you are present you can share your ideas and thoughts."

"Ok, I will in the future. I'm sure the team noticed that I was distracted during the meeting."

"I totally understand why you were distracted. You usually participate actively so it is likely the team noticed something was different. From my perspective, when you are not able to engage in our team meetings we miss out on your contributions. You know that we value and need your good thinking to help the team."

"I appreciate it. I will connect with Lisa and share some thoughts I had after the meeting once I had some time to think about it."

"Amazing, I know she'll appreciate that. And please, if you ever feel like you need to take some time just let me know and we'll make it work."

"That sounds great. Thank you."

This is one example of how the discussion might have gone. I used this as an example because imagine if we would have applied one of the feedback models that we explored earlier to tell John he needs to put his phone down during the meeting and speak up during the team meetings. He may have shut down, begrudgingly agreed, and not shared that he had a family emergency he was dealing with at the time. There could have been a place in this exchange to provide your experience in the meeting as an observation. Some of that was brought in, but given the short and somewhat disengaged responses from John, we took it a different direction. John recognized he was distracted and even came up with an idea without prompting.

Again, this could have gone a lot of different ways, but I just wanted to share a possible way to leverage some of the TALK concepts to try to listen, connect, and explore the situation with curiosity and compassion.

Now What?

A quick reference guide is on the following page to help you gather your thoughts as you prepare and go through the discussion. Use this to note some questions and ideas that you have to direct an exchange of perspectives between you and another person. You will find this helpful in many situations. I have leveraged this approach not just in a professional context but also in my personal life, even finding success with my young sons.

TALK Quick Reference Guide

	Reminders	Your Notes/ Questions
Think *Consider how to approach the discussion and what questions you will ask to ensure an understanding of each other's perspective*	• Test your assumptions • Tune into your own emotions • Trust that the other person has experiences and knowledge • Tact is key to success • Together you can move forward	
Ask *Open the dialogue with a question. Ask for their reflections before sharing yours*	• Agree to the agenda • Align on the goals • Acknowledge their perspectives • Adapt to the conversation flow	

Dynamic Dialogues

Listen *Actively listen to the other person, seek to understand not just to respond*	• Learn what the other person thinks and what matters to them • Logical dialogue is the goal • Look for connections to bridge your perspectives, especially if they are in conflict • Lift the other person	
Know *Knowledge is the ultimate goal of the discussion. Target self-reflection and expanded awareness*	• Keep the dialogue productive • Kindness is crucial • Knit the story together • Kindle their passion • Kudos!	

Conclusion

We defined what feedback is and how it is essential to all humans. Feedback is a biological imperative and required to keep us safe. Put simply, we need feedback to survive.

We discussed the purpose of feedback. We give feedback with the intention of improving another person by helping them see and understand the impact of their actions. We discussed how the principles of feedback are sound in theory but may fall short in application.

We reviewed several different models that help us structure and deliver feedback. Each model having strengths and challenges.

We outlined the different ways feedback is used within organizations to gain insight into how employees are feeling. There are many positives to having a strong employee listening mechanism. There are also many challenges present when deployed organizationally which we touched upon.

We then unveiled the fundamental feedback flaws. Tapping into neuroscience to gain a better understanding of how our brain reacts to feedback. We highlighted why it is so difficult to give or receive feedback and the missteps we make in giving it.

We discovered the lasting impact that feedback can have, particularly on women. We exposed consequences of feedback that may build barriers to being able to effectively listen to and consider other people's perspectives. And how we as humans become conditioned to avoid situations where we may receive feedback.

We considered expert advice on how to improve feedback. In this we found great ideas to move us forward to create a better feedback experience.

We learned about how coaching can address many of the fundamental feedback flaws. We started discussing how to combine feedback and coaching to leverage the best of both approaches.

We brought together the best aspects of feedback and coaching to drive more dynamic dialogues with the intent of exchanging perspectives. We learned how to just talk with each other to gain a deeper understanding of each other and how to create better outcomes together. The intent of sharing perspectives, or giving feedback, is knowledge. It is to expand self-awareness which ultimately reduces the reliance on needing feedback to fill in our blind spots. By taking a more human-centered approach to cultivate dynamic dialogues with people we can reduce the amount of stress and negative consequences of feedback in our personal and professional lives.

I urge you to practice applying these. We know that there are gaps between what we learn and how we apply that learning, after all we're human and bound to make mistakes. Just keep trying to be more empathetic and honor the other person. Success is helping them to come to a solution that works for them. Consider what questions to ask and be curious in the conversation. Don't think about it as "I have to give feedback" or "I am going to have a coaching conversation." Consider it as an opportunity to have a dynamic dialogue and bring in principles and methods from both.

In my experience by approaching my feedback conversations in this way I have been able to get a better sense of how much self-awareness the other person has and whether they need me to share my perspective or have come to a place where they already are aware of the impact they've had. By opening the discussion and allowing the other person to share their thinking, I have been able to test my own observations and opinions.

Remember, humans are emotional creatures, and our brain works to identify and protect us from threats. When we work with neuroscience to expand our approach to incorporate ways to embrace the emotional response and move toward more logic-driven discussions, we can achieve better outcomes for everyone involved.

One last piece of advice before you go. **Assume each person is fully capable of growing and learning.** And adapt your role in that journey for them as you learn what it is they really need from you.

Thank you for reading this book and investing in a more human-centered way to exchange perspectives. I hope that you learned something that will help you have more impactful conversations where you can provide insight to others while taking in their perspective as well. I understand that giving and receiving feedback is hard, and my goal is for you to walk away with a few tips and practical tools to help you navigate the experience.

References

[1] Rock, David, Beth Jones, and Chris Weller. "Using Neuroscience to Make Feedback Work and Feel Better." strategy+business, August 27, 2018. https://www.strategy-business.com/article/Using-Neuroscience-to-Make-Feedback-Work-and-Feel-Better.

[2] Wakim, Suzanne, and Mandeep Grewal. "10.7: Homeostasis and Feedback." Biology LibreTexts. Libretexts, September 4, 2021. https://bio.libretexts.org/Bookshelves/Human_Biology/Book%3A_Human_Biology_(Wakim_and_Grewal)/10%3A_Introduction_to_the_Human_Body/10.7%3A_Homeostasis_and_Feedback.

[3] Betts, J. Gordon, Peter Desaix, Eddie Johnson, Jody E. Johnson, Oksana Korol, Dean Kruse, Brandon Poe, James Wise, Mark D. Womble, and Kelly A. Young. "1.5 Homeostasis." Essay. In *Anatomy and Physiology*. Houston, TX: OpenStax, 2013. https://openstax.org/books/anatomy-and-physiology/pages/1-5-homeostasis.

[4] Sandritaverooka, CC BY-SA 4.0 <https://creativecommons.org/licenses/by-sa/4.0>, via Wikimedia Commons from https://upload.wikimedia.org/wikipedia/commons/5/56/Dibujo_explicativo.jpg.

[5] Gonsalves, Kelly. "This Magic 5:1 Ratio Is the Key To Healthy Relationships, Marriage Experts Say." mindbodygreen, June 14, 2022. https://www.mindbodygreen.com/articles/magic-ratio-in-relationships.

[6] Biggar, Kevin. "Is There a Magic Ratio of Positivity to Negativity?" Kevin Biggar, July 19, 2020. https://www.kevinbiggar.co.nz/blog-is-there-a-magic-ratio-of-positivity-to-negativity/.

[7] Quotemaster. "Think before You Speak. Is It True, Helpful, Inspiring, Necessary, Kind? - Alan Redpath." THINK before you speak. Is it True, Helpful, Inspiring, Necessary, Kind? Alan Redpath. Accessed March 24, 2023. https://www.quotemaster.org/q176ab5b6e598859fa76c4ec06a4fabe7.

[8] Buckingham, Marcus, and Ashley Goodall. "The Feedback Fallacy." *Harvard Business Review*, March 10, 2023. https://hbr.org/2019/03/the-feedback-fallacy.

[9] Chowdhury, Sabrin, Bryan Hancock, and Owain Williams. "Unlocking the True Value of Effective Feedback Conversations." McKinsey & Company, n.d. https://www.mckinsey.com/capabilities/people-and-organizational-performance/our-insights/the-organization-blog/unlocking-the-true-value-of-effective-feedback-conversations.

[10] Bingham, Sue. "More Training Won't Solve Your Company's Problems." *Harvard Business Review*, February 22, 2022. https://hbr.org/2022/02/more-training-wont-solve-your-companys-problems.

[11] Holland, Kimberly. "Amygdala Hijack: When Emotion Takes Over." Edited by Karin Gepp. *Healthline*, Healthline Media, March 16, 2023. https://www.healthline.com/health/stress/amygdala-hijack.

[12] Marshall Lippincott, Jenifer. "Our Brains Are to Blame: The Neuroscience of Feedback." *Training Industry*, February 9, 2018. https://trainingindustry.com/articles/performance-management/our-brains-are-to-blame-the-neuroscience-of-feedback/.

[13] Jones, Paul Anthony. "38 Facts about Shakespeare's 38 Plays." *Mental Floss*. Mental Floss, April 22, 2016. https://www.mentalfloss.com/article/78725/38-facts-about-shakespeares-38-plays.

References

[14] Dirks, Tim. "Best Film Speeches and Monologues 1958-1959." Best film speeches and monologues, n.d. https://www.filmsite.org/bestspeeches18.html#:~:text=Clarence%20Darrow-like%20attorney%20Jonathan,true%20monologue%20in%20film%20history.

[15] Los Angeles Daily News, CC BY 4.0 <https://creativecommons.org/licenses/by/4.0>, via Wikimedia Commons from https://commons.wikimedia.org/wiki/File:Orson_Welles_on_witness_stand_1943.jpg.

[16] Shatz, Itamar. "The Egocentric Bias: Why It's Hard to See Things from a Different Perspective." Effectiviology, n.d. https://effectiviology.com/egocentric-bias/.

[17] "Neural Pathways: How Your Mind Stores the Info and Thoughts that Affect Your Behaviour." LifeXchange, n.d. https://lifexchangesolutions.com/neural-pathways/.

[18] Pyschology Today Staff, ed. "Emotional Intelligence." *Psychology Today*. Sussex Publishers, n.d. https://www.psychologytoday.com/us/basics/emotional-intelligence.

[19] Farnam Street. "Carol Dweck: A Summary of Growth and Fixed Mindsets." FS Blog. Farnam Street, February 5, 2021. https://fs.blog/carol-dweck-mindset/.

[20] Moline, Peg. "We're Far More Afraid of Failure than Ghosts: Here's How to Stare It Down." *Los Angeles Times*. Los Angeles Times, October 31, 2015. https://www.latimes.com/health/la-he-scared-20151031-story.html#:~:text=A%20recent%20survey%20by%20the,even%20the%20paranormal%20(15%25).

[21] Todd, Sarah. "How Negative Feedback Impacts Women and Men Differently." Quartz. Quartz, November 8, 2022. https://qz.com/work/2093763/how-negative-feedback-impacts-women-differently/.

[22] Coffman, Katherine B., Paola Ugalde Araya, and Basit Zafar. "A (Dynamic) Investigation of Stereotypes, Belief-Updating, and

Behavior." National Bureau of Economic Research (NBER), October 18, 2021. https://www.nber.org/papers/w29382.

[23] "David Rock's SCARF Model: Social Threats in the World of Work." The World of Work Project, July 29, 2021. https://worldofwork.io/2019/07/david-rocks-scarf-model/.

[24] Smedley, Mark. "Why Feedback Fails: Your Guide to Effective Feedback at WorkMark." DDI, February 2, 2022. https://www.ddiworld.com/blog/why-feedback-fails.

[25] Lippincott, Jenifer Marshall. "Our Brains Are to Blame: The Neuroscience of Feedback." *Training Industry*, February 9, 2018. https://trainingindustry.com/articles/performance-management/our-brains-are-to-blame-the-neuroscience-of-feedback/.

[26] Lee, D., (2020). "Strengths-Based Team Coaching: Strategies for Intact Teams." (GallupAtWork Virtual Summit June, 2020)

[27] McLain, Denise, and Bailey Nelson. "How Fast Feedback Fuels Performance." Gallup.com. Gallup, January 1, 2022. https://www.gallup.com/workplace/357764/fast-feedback-fuels-performance.aspx.

[28] Borysenko, Karlyn. "Why Giving Feedback at Work Doesn't Improve Performance, and What You Can Do about It." Forbes. *Forbes Magazine*, March 19, 2019. https://www.forbes.com/sites/karlynborysenko/2019/03/19/why-giving-feedback-at-work-doesnt-improve-performance-and-what-you-can-do-about-it/?sh=4d5d81e329ba.

[29] "Leading the Global Advancement of Coaching." International Coaching Federation, March 31, 2023. https://coachingfederation.org/about.

[30] Versino, Melissa. 2022. "Air Force Rolls Out Coaching Culture Facilitator Course Pilot for Mid-Level Leaders." Air Force. October 25, 2022. https://www.af.mil/News/Article-Display/Article/2476355/air-force-rolls-out-coaching-culture-facilitator-course-pilot-for-mid-level-lea/.

References

[31] Unattributed (https://commons.wikimedia.org/wiki/File:Brougham,_19th_century.jpg), Brougham, 19th century, marked as public domain, more details on Wikimedia Commons: https://commons.wikimedia.org/wiki/File:Brougham,_19th_century.jpg.

[32] "Prefrontal Cortex." The Human Memory, March 14, 2022. https://human-memory.net/prefrontal-cortex/.

[33] Gamon, David, and Allen D. Bragdon. Essay. In *Your Brain and What It Does*, Second edition. Allen D. Bragdon Publishers, Inc., 2003. http://www.brainwaves.com/.

[34] Rowden, Adam. "What to Know about Amygdala Hijack." Edited by Joslyn Jelinek. *Medical News Today*. MediLexicon International. Accessed April 19, 2021. https://www.medicalnewstoday.com/articles/amygdala-hijack#signs-and-symptoms.

[35] Musho Hamilton, Diane. "Calming Your Brain During Conflict." *Harvard Business Review*, December 22, 2015. https://hbr.org/2015/12/calming-your-brain-during-conflict.

[36] Brown, Gene. "Difference Between the Amygdala and the Prefrontal Cortex." Difference Between Similar Terms and Objects, April 27, 2021. http://www.differencebetween.net/science/difference-between-the-amygdala-and-the-prefrontal-cortex/.

[37] Hoffeld, David. "Want To Know What Your Brain Does When It Hears A Question?" *Fast Company*, February 21, 2017. https://www.fastcompany.com/3068341/want-to-know-what-your-brain-does-when-it-hears-a-question.

[38] Bosman, Marie. "Self-Directed Neuroplasticity: Change Your Life by Changing Your Focus." Strategic Leadership Institute, August 18, 2021. https://www.stratleader.net/sli-blog/self-directed-neuroplasticity.

Made in the USA
Monee, IL
12 December 2023